# Social Work with Groups
*Mining the Gold*

# THE HAWORTH PRESS
## New, Recent, and Forthcoming
## Titles of Related Interest

# Social Work with Groups
## *Mining the Gold*

Sue Henry
Jean East
Cathryne Schmitz
Editors

The Haworth Press®
New York • London • Oxford

The Haworth Press, Inc., 10 Alice Street, Binghamton, NY 13904-1580.

Cover design by Jennifer M. Gaska.

**Library of Congress Cataloging-in-Publication Data**

Social work with groups : mining the gold / Sue Henry, Jean East, Cathryne Schmitz, editors.
    p. cm.
    Selected proceedings of the 21st annual symposium of the Association for the Advancement of Social Work with Groups, Denver, Colo., Oct. 1999.
    Includes bibliographical references and index.
    ISBN 0-7890-1277-4 (alk. paper) — ISBN 0-7890-1278-2 (alk. paper)
    1. Social group work—Congresses. I. Henry, Sue, 1934- II. East, Jean. III. Schmitz, Cathryne L., 1946- IV. Association for the Advancement of Social Work with Groups. Symposium (21st : 1999 : Denver, Colo.)

HV45 .S644 2002
361.4—dc21

                                         2001043366

# CONTENTS

# ABOUT THE EDITORS

**Jean F. East, PhD,** has written about and worked extensively in empowerment practice. Her research focuses on community-based programs that foster and promote self-sufficiency and empowerment, especially for women. She is cofounder of Project WISE (Women's Initiative for Service and Empowerment) in Denver, Colorado, which was recognized by the El Pomar Foundation as the outstanding nonprofit organization in Colorado in 2000. She is Associate Professor at the University of Denver.

**Sue Henry, DSW,** is Professor Emerita at the University of Denver. Her practice in social group work spans five decades. Her work draws on a social goals/social action framework. Her book, *Group Skills in Social Work,* has been used extensively in the United States and in other countries. She has led group work seminars in Italy and Poland and presented papers at the European Groupwork Symposium in the United Kingdom and Ireland. She chaired Symposium XXI.

**Cathryne L. Schmitz, PhD, ACSW,** is Associate Professor and Director of the Department of Social Work at the University of Southern Maine. Her professional interests include poverty, oppression, diversity, housing, multidisciplinary service delivery, supervision, and management. Much of her teaching, evaluation, research, and scholarship focuses on understanding the issues and needs of low-income, disempowered, multicultural children, families, and communities. She is the co-editor of *Diversity in Single-Parent Families: Working from Strength,* as well as numerous articles.

# CONTRIBUTORS

**Paul Abels,** Professor Emeritus and social activist, received his MSW from Boston University and his PhD from the University of Chicago and was in direct practice with groups and communities prior to teaching. He was Professor and Associate Dean at the (Mandel) School of Applied Social Sciences at Case Western Reserve University in Cleveland. Paul is the former director of the social work program at California State University, Long Beach; author of a number of books and articles; a Fulbright lecturer in Turkey and Iran; and cofounder of a school of social work in Lithuania.

**Sonia Leib Abels** received her MSW from the University of Illinois at Chicago after time as an "untrained group worker" at the YM/YWHA in Newark, New Jersey. She was a Community Action Program trainer in Cleveland during the War on Poverty years and was Group Services Coordinator for Cuyahoga County (Ohio) Child Welfare. She was Associate Professor at Cleveland State University's Department of Social Work and subsequently was a visiting professor at various schools and universities in the United States and abroad. At California State University, Long Beach, Sonia created and edited the journal *Reflections: Narratives of Professional Helping.* Currently she is a member of the journal's board while she undertakes her newest project, "Social Work Practice: Ethics Database."

**Janice T. Cannon** received her BSW from Metropolitan State College in Denver, Colorado, and her MSW from the University of Denver. Janice is employed at the Denver, Colorado, Department of Human Services as a Senior Social Caseworker.

**Patty Crawford** is a resident service coordinator at the Augustana Apartments in Minneapolis, Minnesota. In this 380-unit senior complex, she assists in accessing services, and facilitates grief and loss support groups, a writing group, a reminiscence group, and an exercise program. She has twenty-five years of experience working with the elderly. Patty is a graduate of Augsburg College in Minneapolis, Minnesota.

**Robin Edward Gearing** is the father of two wonderful children. He works as a family and group therapist focusing on strengthening family systems with specific attention to the roles of fathers and mothers.

**Erin Gingerich** received a BS from Goshen College in Goshen, Indiana. Following graduation, she worked as a home-base manager for Elkhart County, Indiana, and then attended the University of Denver from which she received her MSW. Erin is now employed at Denver Health Medical Center as Case Manager, social worker for Pediatric Services and Pediatric Intensive Care Unit.

**Jacqueline B. Helfgott** is Associate Professor of Criminal Justice in the Department of Sociology and Criminal Justice at Seattle University. Her research interests include institutional and community corrections, the psychopathic personality, crime and popular culture, deviance and social control, and restorative justice. She has been involved in the implementation and evaluation of the Citizens, Victims, and Offenders Restoring Justice Program at the Washington State Reformatory (a restorative-justice-oriented prison program funded through the Center on Crime, Communities, and Culture of the Open Society Institute). In addition to teaching and research, she is the coordinator for the Creative Expressions Project, a volunteer prison program at both the Washington State Reformatory and the Washington Correctional Center for Women, which involves offenders in community-oriented writing and art projects.

**Carol S. Hinote** is a certified social worker and registered art therapist. With many years of experience leading therapy groups and supervising group therapists, she directs a family counseling site within a Brooklyn, New York, middle school. She is also a professional photographer, with a University of Michigan MFA in Photography, whose work was most recently shown at a one-person Madison, Wisconsin, exhibit in the summer of 2000.

**Linda Hutton, CSW,** is a staff psychotherapist at the Fifth Avenue Center for Counseling and Psychotherapy and also has a private practice in Manhattan, New York. She is a candidate at the National Institute for Psychotherapies in Manhattan and a doctoral student at Fordham University, New York.

**Charles Lawrence, PhD,** is Associate Professor of Sociology, Chair of the Sociology Department, and Associate Dean of Arts and Sciences for Student Affairs at Seattle University.

**Nuala Lordan** is a senior lecturer in the Department of Applied Social Studies at University College in Cork, Ireland, where she also carries several departmental administrative assignments. She holds a BSocSc and DipSocSc as well as an MSW from the United States. In addition to her teaching duties, Nuala is an advocate and activist in the vanguard of many movements fighting social injustice. With her co-author, Nuala has worked, trained, and taught tirelessly throughout Europe and the European Union, using social group work skills to combat social exclusion.

**Madeline L. Lovell, MSW, PhD,** is Associate Professor in the Department of Sociology and Criminal Justice at Seattle University. She directs the social work program there. She currently holds the Gaffney Endowed Chair for Jesuit Identity and Mission in the College of Arts and Sciences with the goal of fostering faculty analyses of complex social problems and possible interventions. Her major mode of practice is group work.

**Susan S. Manning, PhD,** has focused her research efforts on empowerment models for people who suffer from serious psychiatric disability. She teaches indirect practice theories, professional ethics, and qualitative research methods at the University of Denver Graduate School of Social Work. She is particularly interested in the integration of empowerment models and group approaches in direct and indirect interventions.

**Ellen Sue Mesbur** is Professor at the School of Social Work at Ryerson Polytechnic University in Toronto, where she was Director of the School for nine years. Her teaching and scholarly interests include social group work practice, gerontological social work practice, and field education; she has published and presented papers internationally at many symposia and conferences. She chaired both the Ontario and Canadian Committees of Deans and Directors of Schools of Social Work and is a member of the Board of Accreditation of the Canadian Association of Schools of Social Work. Currently she is Co-chairperson of the 22nd Annual International Symposium for the Advancement of Social Work with Groups in Toronto.

**Ruth J. Parsons, PhD,** retired in 2000 as Professor in the Graduate School of Social Work at the University of Denver. Building on her early group work foundation, she has been engaged in the development of empowerment practice theory for the past fifteen years. She continues to pursue research and scholarship in empowerment and involvement in the development of social work education in China and the West Indies.

**Sandra Regan, MSW, EdM, PhD,** is a senior lecturer at the University of New South Wales' School of Social Work in Sydney, Australia. She has extensive experience in teaching group work and leading a wide range of face-to-face and teleconferencing groups in a variety of settings. She has a particular interest in exploring the links between theory and practice in teleconferencing groups and developing innovative ways of using teleconferencing as part of the helping process to reach geographically dispersed populations.

**Marshall Rubin, LCSW, ACSW,** lives in Tucson, Arizona. He is currently President of Marshall Rubin and Associates, Inc., and provides consultation and training in social group work and supervisory practices. He is a founder and past president of the International Association of Psychosocial Rehabilitation Services.

**Beverly S. Ryan** earned an MSW from the University of St. Thomas/ College of St. Catherine in St. Paul, Minnesota. She has twenty-one years of social work experience in both individual and group work with the elderly. Her areas of expertise span the nursing home, senior housing, home care, hospital, and hospice environments. Beverly is currently employed in Oncology Services at United Hospital within the Allina Health System, St. Paul, Minnesota.

**Nancy Sullivan, PhD,** has taught social work at the University of Toronto, Ryerson Polytechnic University, and at Renison College at the University of Waterloo, with an earlier practice career in child welfare. She has been an active member of the Toronto Region Group-workers' Network (the Toronto Chapter of AASWG), serving on the local Executive Committee and on the International AASWG Board and several of its committees. She was Co-chairperson of the AASWG Symposium held in Toronto in 2000.

**Mary Wilson** is a lecturer in the Department of Applied Social Studies at University College in Cork, Ireland. She holds a BSocSc and DSWS (from Glasgow), as well as a PhD and a CQSW. Mary's commitment to social justice is evident in the work she does throughout Ireland and the remainder of Europe. As does her co-author, Mary works with training, and teaches about social exclusion, using social group work skills as the principal instrument for addressing the issue.

# Preface

The chapters in this volume represent a sampling of the presentations at Symposium XXI of the Association for the Advancement of Social Work with Groups, Inc., an International, Professional Organization, which took place in Denver, Colorado, in October 1999. Those attending the symposium were enthusiastic about the variety of topics offered. All of the papers and plenary sessions were thought-provoking and stimulating. From the opening session by Nuala Lordan and Mary Wilson, our colleagues from Ireland, to the incisive folk music of the evening, to the Friday luncheon plenary session by recent MSW graduates Janice Cannon and Erin Gingerich in the aftermath of the shootings at suburban Columbine High School, to the closing session by Denver empowerment theorists Jean East, Susan Manning, and Ruth Parsons, all of the plenary sessions showed the power of social group work to address problems. Between and among the plenaries, the various papers, workshops, and invitationals gave good evidence of the efficacy of our practice method. Pre-symposium institutes challenged practice, research, education, and theory development.

The co-editors of this volume, Jean East and Cathryne Schmitz, each had roles in the symposium. Jean East copresented a symposium session on her work in a community-based empowerment and self-sufficiency program, and she was one of the presenters at the closing plenary on the interface between the empowerment agenda and social group work. Cathryne Schmitz, at the time a member of the faculty at the Graduate School of Social Work at the University of Denver, was the principal actor in steering the abstracts review process for the symposium. In her capacity as a co-editor of this volume, her involvement in Symposium XXI and with the chapters comes full circle.

Authors were invited to introduce themselves to readers in their own words. Those introductions are found in the Contributors pages. Worth mention here is the fact that the editors made accuracy of citations and consistency of style the responsibility of the authors themselves. The editors did not take on the burden of editing copy. The editing that occurred was done either by the authors or by the editing staff at The Haworth Press. The editors express deep appreciation to Patricia Brown at Haworth for her guidance and support through this process.

In the end, Symposium XXI truly showed all that is golden about social group work, and we are very happy to share that with you.

*Sue Henry, DSW*
*Professor Emerita*
*Senior Editor*

# Introduction

The Twenty-First Annual Symposium of the Association for the Advancement of Social Work with Groups, held in Denver, Colorado, was the last symposium of the twentieth century and represented a unique moment for looking back to our roots and for looking forward to the twenty-first century. The theme, "Mining the Gold in Social Work with Groups," represented this transition time.

Mining was part of the growth of Colorado, and its remnants are scattered across the Colorado landscape in a state that represents a postmodern world: technology-based growth, youth violence in the suburbs, international connections, and downtown revitalization—while the homeless sleep in new urban parks. Mining is about exploration, looking for precious minerals in the earth. A structure is sometimes built, underground or across streams, to allow miners to go farther to find gold. Symposium XXI represented such a process. Social group work has a long and rich history in the social work profession—and in Colorado as well. The standards and practice of social group work are built on theory and practice evidence, a structure that provides a supporting foundation.

How can we continue to strengthen this foundation and yet stay relevant in the twenty-first century? How can we preserve the treasures of social group work and yet make the most of work with groups in the postmodern world? These questions form the backdrop for the symposium and the chapters in this collection. Some chapters represent traditional uses of groups and their efficacy in working with oppressed populations. Others take emerging social work traditions such as empowerment and dig further into the meanings of those concepts in the practice of social group work. Finally, new ideas are proposed that can advance social work with groups into the future. Each of the chapters represents a commitment to social group work as an important method in social work practice.

## PLENARY SESSIONS

The three plenary sessions of the symposium represented a range of perspectives that embodied "mining the gold" in social work with groups. The opening banquet address by Nuala Lordan and Mary Wilson was titled, "Groupwork in Europe: Tools to Combat Social Exclusion in a Multicultural Environment." The address focused on the authors' experiences in educating social work students to use group work as a tool for combating social exclusion in Europe. The presentation was thoughtful and challenging and provided participants with a model for teaching group work that is relevant to issues of oppression and multiculturalism in the world today. It also keeps us mindful of the real-life matters faced by people of other nations and cultures and of the role of social work elsewhere in the world.

The second plenary, at the Friday luncheon, was titled "Seeking Alternatives to Violence: A School-Based Violence Prevention Project." This session was an outgrowth of the University of Denver Graduate School of Social Work's response to the Columbine High School violence in April 1999. As one can imagine, the Columbine shootings touched many of us personally and professionally. Those of us on the faculty at DU found ourselves in endless conversations with students on the meaning of the event and the possibilities for a social work response. Ironically, the news came to some of us at DU while we were in a class on empowerment practice. As a result of our discussions in that class, two graduate students decided to apply the principles of empowerment practice to a proposed intervention for the prevention of school violence.

The luncheon keynote began with a presentation from Fred Garcia, coordinator of the Colorado educational systems' responses to the Columbine shootings. During his remarks, he acknowledged the presence at the symposium luncheon of Dr. Del Elliott from the University of Colorado, founder and director of the Center for the Study and Prevention of Violence and internationally known expert on the study of violence. This was followed by Janice Cannon and Erin Gingerich's presentation of their work. The program they designed, Seeking Alternative Solutions to Violence, included a student-focused and student-directed community empowerment model that would seek to empower youth. While the presentation and the ideas were just a beginning and need to be developed more fully, the work represents a solid effort on the part of graduate students to put ideas into practice.

The closing plenary session, presented by Jean East, Susan Manning, and Ruth Parsons, was a fitting wrap-up to the rich variety of papers and presentations of the symposium. The session was titled "The Social Work Empowerment Agenda and Social Work with Groups." The session began with a presentation by Parsons on the principles and research on empowerment practice. This was followed by an interactive session with participants who gave input on the supports and challenges to putting into practice empowerment principles with different types of groups. The chapter included in this volume synthesizes the material presented and the group input. There was great energy in this session and the "gold" of social group work was evident in the rich responses of experience and practice wisdom expressed.

## SYMPOSIUM PRESENTATIONS

Setting the tone, Paul and Sonia Abels challenge us to think beyond the known. In the postmodern, reconstructive era they describe, no approach should be "privileged" over others "without examination of its value." Their chapter and others in this volume provide many models of social group work, some traditional and some new and creative, but none more privileged or valued than others. In "Narrative Social Work with Groups: Just in Time," the Abelses present a "natural" approach, incorporating and centering clients' lives and views. They describe a "liberating" model with value across cultures and environments. Clients are valued and empowered as they explore their lives and examine their own problems. The use of narratives surfaces again in Madeline Lovell, Jacqueline Helfgott, and Charles Lawrence's "Citizens, Victims, and Offenders Restoring Justice: A Prison-Based Group Work Program Bridging the Divide." Personal crime narratives become a healing tool in a restorative justice program. It is an innovative model with the potential to reempower the isolated and disenfranchised.

Robin Edward Gearing's discussion in "Gender Diversity: A Powerful Tool for Enriching Group Experience" explores another area that has received little attention in the group work literature. He explores the power and strength in diversity, discussing the implications for enhancing and enriching practice. In Carol Hinote's "Group Work with Minority Mentally Ill Men: The Role of the Woman Worker," the impact of gender and cultural differences between worker and group participants is explored. The author proposes that cross-gender work may help move us beyond ill-fitting gender stereotypes.

"Building Bridges Over Troubled Waters: A Bridging Model for Teleconferencing Group Counselling" by Sandra Regan links the technological and the human. In this new era, electronic connections offer new potential for connecting the geographically and physically isolated. This exciting chapter describes the integration of techniques from multiple models into a new form with benefit for connecting across electronic bridges. Teaching social group work through the use of simulated group experience is explored and evaluated in Nancy Sullivan and Ellen Sue Mesbur's "Groupworkers in the Making: A Simulation for Teaching Social Groupwork." This teaching technique provides an experiential learning opportunity that is multi-dimensional and interactional. Through involvement in the practice simulation, skills and knowledge are integrated as the foundation for student growth.

Models of practice with special populations are explored in the final three chapters. In "Creating Loss Support Groups for the Elderly" by Beverly Ryan and Patty Crawford, the challenges and strengths of working with loss support groups in senior housing are reviewed. The authors explore the negative consequences of focusing service development on weakness rather than strength. The importance of supporting the grief process is examined. As elders share in an open grief process, new opportunities open up.

The use of "curriculum-driven" groups is increasing, leading to a crisis in the implementation of services, according to Marshall Rubin. In "Making Curriculum Purposeful in Group Work with Persons with Severe Mental Illness," Rubin examines and critiques the "curriculum-driven" model through comparison with the mutual aid model of group work. He presents a model for using curriculum with purpose, integrating the principles and skills of mutual aid practice to develop effective models of group work practice.

Linda Hutton's "Reflecting Extremes of Human Experience in the Group: Work with Chemically Addicted Chronic Paranoid Schizophrenic Clients" describes another application of a group work model with participants struggling with multiple barriers resulting from mental illness and chemical addiction.

The chapters in this volume are far-ranging. Theory, vision, creativity, and challenge coexist with description and analysis. Centering client stories, recognizing and valuing diversity, and focusing on gender and empowerment are discussions bringing us into a new century. Implementation and evaluation of traditional and innovative models with a range of populations provide the reader with knowledge and ideas for mining the gold in social group work.

*Jean East, PhD*
*Cathryne Schmitz, PhD*
*Co-Editors*

# PART I:
# PLENARY SESSIONS

Chapter 1

# Groupwork in Europe:
# Tools to Combat Social Exclusion
# in a Multicultural Environment

Nuala Lordan
Mary Wilson

Without contraries is no progression.

William Blake,
"The Marriage of Heaven and Hell"

## *INTRODUCTION*

We are delighted to be with you in Denver, the Mile High City, beginning the process of mining the gold. A quotation from W. B. Yeats aptly encompasses this reality by suggesting that "between extremities, man runs his course" (Yeats, 1933, p. 283).

This chapter focuses on some of our experiences in educating social work students to use groupwork as a tool for combating social exclusion in Europe. We will draw on the experiences of seminar students from very different social and cultural milieus in order to tease out some conceptual truths. We will also explore the many challenges of working in a multicultural and multilingual environment, using some of the techniques that the students found most beneficial to their learning. Finally, we will discuss the applications of the approach in the wider sphere of social action to relate its relevance to other contexts.

## EDUCATION AND TRANSFORMATION

Knowledge is not value-free; it tends to reflect the values and attitudes of the giver and the context in which it is promulgated. Neither is the dissemination of knowledge static; it is a dynamic engagement of dialogue and reflection that builds toward thinking in critically analytic ways. This has implications for the reality offered by our universities, where the emphasis is on coherence and conformity, often at the expense of complexity and chaos. Do we foster critical, creative complexity (a simplistic divide) or value coherence, which may harbour conformity? Coherence and complexity need not be at variance; they are mutually reinforcing, two sides of the same coin. But often they are considered to be mutually exclusive. In this respect, our academic institutions may constitute a reality where coherence and conformity are achieved at the expense of complexity and chaos. Instead, an educational forum is required where the learner's knowledge and experience is valued and received knowledge is exposed to critical scrutiny. Here Blake's quotation provides an apt summary: "The tigers of wrath are wiser than the horses of instruction" (Erdman, 1988, p. 37).

### Using Groups to Transform Education

Groupwork, we believe, can provide such an educational environment. Groups have long been recognised as a major forum for learning. From the initial and tentative social learning made by the individual in the family, the process continues over each person's lifetime by means of the various groups in which he or she is involved. This definition of groupwork locates it in the broader sphere of socially constructed knowledge or social education and brings with it the possibility of transformation. Practice and pedagogical dimensions are included in this view. Practice wisdom suggests that the outcome of any intervention is predicated on and determined by the perspective from which it is directed. We believe that the knowledge that learning is socially constructed is a fundamental prerequisite for practice intervention, which recognises the individual's unique model of knowledge building (Gergen, 1985; Goldstein, 1990; Real, 1990). Groupwork offers a way to overcome the theory-practice dissonance, which has contributed to the maintenance of the "culture gap" between the academic and practice areas of the work. In this way, groupwork provides a synthesis to promote a transformative analysis. Thus group-work challenges traditional pedagogical learning principles by representing "the personal is political" perspective, which locates it at the "coalface" of liberation and feminist approaches to education.

## *Challenging Oppression*

Fundamental to this approach is the focus on challenging injustice and oppression at many levels. Groupwork, in this broad sense, operates primarily in the cultural sphere and has a central role to play in the promotion of inclusive strategies. Education through groupwork, we believe, can be central to the process of empowering socially excluded groups. Huff and Johnson (1988) talk in terms of teaching empowerment through modeling it in their relationships with students in the classroom. These encounters can then mirror the relationships between social workers and clients. In both cases, the relationships are unequal. In both groups, facilitators have implicit power over students and clients. It is important that facilitators acknowledge the reality of this power relationship and try to transform it creatively.

This alternative worldview can be promoted by pushing the boundaries outward. We believe that the process of transforming the potentially oppressive impact of unequal power relationships begins with an explicit acknowledgement of how that power is being used and being open to sharing it and changing its outcome. Transferring and transforming power relationships is central to the view of the world with which we wish our students to engage and encounter. Democratic ideals and practices are integral to this approach. Democratic leadership within an antioppressive framework aims to foster an ethos of student involvement and participation, which facilitates the learning-through-action process. This is challenging for all concerned. Both mentors and students are engaged equally in the process of how and what is taught and learned. An antioppressive framework recognises the importance of naming differences as a first step to understanding them. These differences include gender, race, age, ability, culture, religion, and class. By naming and engaging with these differences from the outset, a culture of liberation can be fostered which is predicated on celebrating and validating difference in partnership with the group. This refers to the process of transforming the democratic ideal into its practice wisdom reality.

## BACKGROUND OF THE EUROPEAN SEMINAR

The seminar brings together students and teachers from different European states for an intensive programme of two weeks' duration. Funding is provided by the Socrates initiative under the auspices of the European Union. The Socrates programme is specifically directed at third-level educational institutions throughout the EU to provide a forum for the sharing of knowledge, research, and expertise among member states. Partnerships are developed by interested faculty who define the area of study and create a programme. This is submitted for funding approval to the EU. In this instance, the proposing group included educationalists from Greece, Ireland, Norway, Spain, and from two universities in the United Kingdom.

The aims of these programmes from an EU perspective are to foster social cohesion and create a European identity. These aims are perceived as important in the process of breaking down national barriers and fostering a cooperative spirit of understanding among the intelligentsia and future leaders in the new Europe. By bringing together young people in the educational institutions of member countries to share and to learn from each other, the belief is that future stability of the United States of Europe can be promoted. Many of these young people believe passionately in ideas of equality and inclusion. This vision of a social Europe is a historical and recurrent concern of European relations. As Europe is still at the stage of defining its identity, a desired outcome of the programme is to foster the students' recognition of their countries' shared characteristics.

### Objectives

Specifically, the purpose of this intensive programme is to enable social work students to explore theoretical models and methods which promote social inclusion. It focuses on the wider use of social groupwork for social action and social change activities as a means of counteracting oppression and social exclusion. As the borders open up between countries through the mobility of labour, it is important that practitioners using the approach learn and work together. The objectives are, first, to assist students in developing an understanding of the manifestation of oppression in their own countries; second, to explore theoretical models to promote social inclusion; and third, to develop innovative responses and explore strategies which lead to inclusion. These objectives are achieved through sharing positive initiatives and examples from each country. By bringing this work together in a transnational teaching and learning forum, it is possible to develop a partnership of relevant theoretical analyses and practice approaches, which are rooted in a trans-European understanding. The approach is based on learning-by-doing strategies. Promoting experiential learning in a multilingual workshop thus provides the basis for developing communication and understanding of the different cultures represented.

## *Structure*

Selection of students to participate in the programme is carried out on a lottery basis from among those who volunteer. Each of the participating colleges is allocated student places, which are based on their overall student numbers. An essential criterion for those who are selected is that they should have some knowledge of English.

The programme has three distinct phases. The first phase takes place at the students' home institutions, where they are engaged in the preplanning stage. The second phase, which is the major part of the programme, consists of an intensive seminar when all the student groups gather at one location in Europe. Participating colleges take turns hosting this event. The final phase of the programme is when the students return home to share their learning with the rest of their student group.

## PRACTICE PRINCIPLES

A number of practice principles are embedded in the facilitation of these student groups. They are as follows:

## *Person Focussed*

This approach recognises the dignity of the whole person. The difference of each individual, their soul, their way of being, experience, and understanding is unique. Difference is a double-edged sword. It can be a cause for celebration as minority groups name and reframe their status in positive terms such as "gay pride" or "black is beautiful." The other edge can cut deep, exposing rejection, hostility, and oppression. Our approach, although recognising the hurt, focuses on celebrating the uniqueness and richness of our differences.

## Working from Strengths

The literature abounds with examples of strengths-based approaches, which emphasise the importance of positive orientation to those with whom we engage. These approaches, such as feminist, self-directed, and empowerment-oriented practice models cohere in emphasising the importance of focusing on strengths rather than problems. Saleebey (1996, p. 297) articulates this practice model by stating, "All must be seen in the light of their capabilities, talents, competencies, possibilities, vision, values, and hopes, however dashed and distorted these may have become through circumstance, oppression and trauma." This accords with our belief that all people are therefore equal in their ability to contribute positively to the group.

## Assigning Equal Value to Process and Outcome

The transformative nature of the process focuses on supporting each person's contribution to the whole. Such holism facilitates differential levels of involvement in the planning and implementation of the programme and is recognised in the group's finding of each individual's capacity to plan, to implement, and to achieve.

> Since a great deal of what is learned . . . occurs outside of the planned formal curriculum (e.g., students learning from each other; the growth of self awareness through group interaction, etc.), it is sensible to process these processes, thence tapping into a rich source of extra learning. (Coulshed, 1993, p. 12)

## Partnership Leading to Ownership

In this approach to groupwork, members are in joint control of the process from the outset. This is a core value, as it gives a choice to the members to become and stay involved in activities that interest them. Social constructionist methodologies support this premise. Stone's principles for classroom empowerment denote a similar emphasis (Stone, 1995, p. 294).

## CREATING REAL DIALOGUE

### *Processing the Personal Perspective*

A richness of this programme is that while the students share the common aim of social work training, they are coming from varied training and practice traditions in social work. It is also likely that there may be a mix of undergraduate and postgraduate students who have very different levels of experience of the role of social work in society. This provides a stimulating and challenging environment in which to work.

On the first day of the programme, as with any beginning group, the focus is on developing trust and helping the group to bond. It is during this process that students are encouraged to be in touch with their personal experience of oppression. The first step is the development of communication. As Sue Henry has stated, "The energy on which groups run is communication, verbal and nonverbal" (Sue Henry, 1981, p. 16). This is recognised as good practice and takes on a special significance when working in a multilingual environment. With this kind of group, it is important from the outset to acknowledge the challenges and difficulties posed by operating in a language which is not one's native tongue.

The students who participate have a number of "given" commonalities when they first engage with the programme. These external factors include their status as social groupwork students, the requirement that they have a working knowledge of the English language, and the fact that they are members of the European Union. From these scant commonalities, the students begin to work toward an acknowledgement that they have more in common than they have dividing them. At this stage in the programme, the emphasis is on helping students to own these similarities, so that they can engage more easily in the process of encountering their differences constructively. Students are then encouraged to deconstruct their stereotypes and personal assumptions of other cultures and traditions, so that they can create better understanding and communicate more meaningfully with each other.

The students enter the programme with an intellectual understanding of marginalisation, discrimination, and oppression. According to Howe, "To a considerable degree, what one 'sees' in social life is dependent upon particular perspectives" (Howe, 1980, in Sheppard, 1995, p. 266). Immediately upon commencing the programme, the facilitators operationalise a process of awakening, which gives emotional content to cerebral material. This results in the development of a context in which oppression is made real. We achieve this by challenging the oppressive nature of the dominant language, in this case, English. The dangers of "colonisation" by English speakers are very real. The non–English-speaking students are aware of and concerned about this. Their recognition of this possible oppression gives substance to their conceptual understandings, and, consequently, it becomes a real and felt experience. When students become aware of the oppressive nature of the predominance of English, they find themselves cast in the role of oppressors and oppressed. Both are very uncomfortable with this "felt" position. They are surprised to feel this so keenly. Consequently, they become highly motivated to find a solution to this dilemma.

As facilitators, we use this experience as an opportunity to encourage the development of a common nonlanguage of gestures, symbols, and actions. Through these nonverbal means of expression, the students are brought closer to a more real awareness of what it is like to be marginalised. We recognise the oppressive power of the language, and we seek to transform it by creating a "wordless language." This transmuted language becomes the means by which the students can gain an understanding of what it is like to be oppressed. It is based on the belief that images rather than words can be closer to our true feelings, even our subconscious feelings, since the process of "thinking with our hands" can short-circuit the censorship of the brain (Boal, 1992).

To continue the process of inclusion, we create a common language or means of communication by using simulation exercises and nonverbal encounters such as sculptures and depictions of their cultural identities and geopolitical relationships. These exercises facilitate the process of identifying commonalities, helping the different student groups to cohere so that national boundaries become blurred and the larger seminar group begins to emerge. One of the students summed this up well by commenting, "I could clearly identify the various groups in the room at any one time. I felt that there was also a very strong sense of an overall larger combined group. I was amazed at how quickly and easily people seemed to merge into this larger group, interacting with one another."

From this position of safety, we begin their exploration and engagement with difference. Difference must be scaffolded so that structural inequalities are exposed. In this intensive programme, differences nationally and linguistically are very obvious and therefore easier to identify. It is our experience that it is much easier to engage and acknowledge one's inability to understand in a situation where vast differences are apparent than with a group where a greater degree of similarity exists. It is the degree of difference which forces us to face and acknowledge our lack of understanding. We agree with Gurevitch when he states, "Students may need help in developing the ability to not understand and in recognising an inability to not understand" (Gurevitch, 1989, p. 164). An important task for social work students is recognising their inability to understand and validating this as a prerequisite to real dialogue and communication.

We expose and build on this initial understanding of nonunderstanding to deepen the sense of commonality from which difference can continue to be safely explored. "The building blocks of meaning making are, for the most part, found in the edifice of culture. Culture provides the means by which people receive, organise, rationalise and understand their experiences of the world" (Saleebey, 1996, p. 301). We facilitate this process by means of action-reflection exercises.

### Processing the Cultural Arena

This moves us to the second level of processing oppression, which focuses student's attention on the cultural arena. It is at this stage that we draw the students' attention to the cultural dimensions of seeing, thinking, and doing. Their first task is to create a map of Europe by locating themselves, without speaking, around the room in spatial relationship to each other, virtually depicting the geophysical construction of the continent. This liberates the creative energy in the group. The movement of finding their location engages them in real terms in the search for their roles. Next, we get them to present themselves "stereotypically," as they believe they are seen by other nationalities. The groups usually respond with gusto to this activity: the Norwegians transform themselves into Vikings, setting out to plunder and pillage or to discover America; the Irish present themselves by dancing a jig; the Spanish relax on the beach. All of this dramatising causes great hilarity and contributes to the bonding and trust-building processes. Finally, they are asked to present a moving tableau of their countries' relationship with the European Union. This challenges the students to focus on and represent the political and structural elements in their environment. Thus the Germans become the paymasters of Europe, miming the giving of money to the other countries. Those on the periphery such as Norway role-play independence and/or ambivalence, while Ireland, Greece, and Spain portray dependence and/or enslavement by a role-play of dancing to the tune paid for by the Germans. In the best traditions of Euro-scepticism, the British feign indifference and/or aloofness by depicting the drinking of tea.

## *Processing Structural Understandings*

Here we reach the final level of the PCS model, which is concerned with the development of structural understandings of oppression. The current European emphasis on creating cohesion can militate against engaging with the difficulties of difference. By seeking to create an ethos of conformity, we deny the innately oppressive substance and form of our socially constructed reality. In this way, these inequalities are embedded in hegemony of orthodoxy, something that as educators we believe should be named and resisted. The rarefied nature of the academic environment militates against the expression of feeling as well as nonrational and nonverbal ways of knowing.

The complexities of social inclusion, however, cannot simply be confined to the realm of academic discourse but must also be addressed by affirmative action programs. Transformative learning, or "conscientization" (Freire, 1970), is a concept that grounds us in the multicultural contexts within which we live and work while signalling the opportunities present in our civilisation. Such possibilities include the capacity to create more democratic forms of our social worlds, the process that Professor Anthony Giddens (1998) calls "democratising democracy."

Real understanding of oppression means encountering it at a feeling level that is beyond knowledge and words. When the students have begun to feel some of the impact of oppression at both the personal and the cultural levels, we move the focus of the exercise to encourage them to look outside themselves at the excluded and marginalised members of their own societies.

To illustrate this concept, we introduce an exercise that touches on the reality of exclusion. It is entitled "Opportunity: Chance or Choice?" The exercise is conducted in total silence. It allocates to participants a series of roles that represent the span of social positions in society. Therefore, roles such as a sixteen-year-old black disabled woman; a forty-year-old wealthy man with AIDS; a seventy-five-year-old disabled widow; and a white, professional, middle-class male, aged thirty are all included to suggest the diversity of society.

Participants are asked to stand in a line with their backs to a wall. They are then asked a series of questions, which they must answer in role. These questions are based on standard expectations of choice and opportunities in life, such as: Can you easily get a loan to buy your own house? Can you easily go on holidays? Can you use public transport or can you drive a car? Can you feel safe walking the streets after dark? Can you easily kiss your lover in public?

If the answer to the question is affirmative, the person in role may take one step forward. If negative, the participant is required to remain where he or she is. Each student is required to respond to each question. As the exercise progresses, the physical space between participants becomes obvious, signifying the inequitable nature of choice and opportunity in society. Students are then asked to share their assigned roles publicly. The discussion then focuses on the movement that they have made, and the feelings that have been generated as a result are identified. Students who have been left behind normally experience feelings of frustration, anger, and hopelessness. They are encouraged to discuss these feelings and reflect on their meanings. This process enables comparisons to be made between commonalities and differences which exist in the different countries. Marginalisation becomes glaringly apparent in the sense that the same people are left behind, left out, excluded as a result of socially sanctioned norms.

It is important that sufficient time is allocated to discuss the issues that arise and to facilitate the sharing of cultural differences. The students divide into multicultural groups. Their task is to identify commonly oppressed groups in society and to present nonverbally what it feels like to be a member of any such marginalised group. Some of the common themes portrayed are poverty, ethnicity, migration, sexuality, power, and powerlessness. These interpretations are deconstructed through discussion of the commonalities and differences inherent in European society. Students begin to identify the relationship between politics and oppression.

## DECONSTRUCTING CONFLICT

At each stage of the group's work, particularly during the discussion of difference, conflict is real and apparent. Students' expression of contentious and competing ideas and behaviours generate an energy which requires discussion, negotiation, and, on occasion, mediation. However, it is our belief that because the emphasis on difference is so overtly acknowledged from the outset, the participants feel and act less defensively and consequently have a greater sense of self-direction.

If it is accepted that we are unable to understand each other, there is a tacit acceptance of conflict as an integral and normal part of the group process. This then facilitates the resolution of conflict without acceleration to hostile levels. "Although conflicts inevitably arise, skilful group facilitation can help avoid unnecessary conflicts and resolve disagreements before they turn into hostile disputes" (Toseland and Rivas, 1998, p. 115). In one group, conflict was expressed vociferously by some members in relation to differing interpretations of the basic philosophy of the programme. This group held a different understanding of power relationships and their implications for practice. The group's presentations and participation were based on this interpretation. When challenged by other subgroups, the students showed themselves initially resistant to the blandishments of dialogue. However, skillful and well-timed intervention by the facilitator, encouraged members to reexamine their inability to understand, and validated this position. Thus it became possible for those under pressure to release feelings of threat that had generated hostility and enabled the establishment of a cooperative group atmosphere.

## THE GROUP TAKES OWNERSHIP

By now the students are fully involved in the working stage of the group. They begin to take ownership by assuming control. To quote from one group of students, "The most striking thing is how the teachers pulled out without the group being aware of it. Suddenly it just felt very natural to take over the organisation of practical issues such as when the different countries should make their presentations. It is very clear that the teachers had succeeded in creating a relaxed informal setting." These student presentations focus on developing the students' awareness and understanding of the paradigm and theoretical diversity of social work in different cultures and social welfare systems. The students from each country make a presentation to all the others in which they review the diversity of welfare provision in their various countries. This ranges from the total welfare state of northern Europe through the mixed economies of welfare which characterise the western European states to the minimalist provision in the south. Included in the presentations is a review and analysis of social action groupwork projects in each country. This contributes to the building of students' confidence and competence in policy analysis and action, fostering a greater openness to exploring more deeply and celebrating the richness of diversity in this multicultural group. "The greater insight that comes from the recognition of diversities in the context of commonalties is rooted in genuine contact with, and perception with the other person" (Hanmer and Statham, 1992, p. 94).

By the end of the week, the students completely own the group process, to the extent that they "forget" that facilitation has been a feature of the experience. This is often demonstrated at the end of the seminar, when they are so involved in the process of closure that they thank each other for the experience and congratulate themselves on a job well done. The role played by the facilitators goes unacknowledged! That the members had moved from an experience of facilitation as "us and them" to one of "we" is a measure of good facilitation. The facilitation was so seamless that they only remembered its input when reviewing what they had learned at the evaluation stage.

This sense of ownership is usually most apparent at the final party, which occurs on the last evening of the seminar and is the social highlight of these events. Students from all the countries prepare and cook their national dishes, which are served with pride and devoured with relish. These social occasions have an equal importance in the life of the programme in that they break down barriers and allow all participants to "play" and make an active contribution to the group task and maintenance of relationships. Some of the greatest learning can take place in these informal and fun situations.

## EVALUATION AND OUTCOME

Students are required to participate in an evaluation session as part of the closure of the programme. In keeping with good practice, this facilitates an ending and letting go. The students are provided with an evaluation sheet to complete by asking for feedback from each other. This form of evaluation has the dual purpose of eliciting empirical evidence and providing a forum in which personal closure can be achieved and future learning signposted.

An important outcome of the seminar for the students lies in their recognition of the exercise of power and its impact. For those who participate, actually having power to make decisions is experienced internally as renewed well-being and externally is reflected in an aura of power suffusing and surrounding their personal and professional encounters. "Walking Tall" encapsulates the idea that we wish to express. It refers to the person's assertion of their right to view the world and to behave in accordance with these beliefs. This way of being is currently supported by the dominant cultural and societal norms.

As an outcome, the students recognise that multiculturalism challenges those universalising norms which regulate meaning and determine truth and value to be neutral. Therefore, working in a multicultural-multilingual environment is real and challenging for them. The aspects of the method that they identify as being most helpful to their learning come from those experiences, which facilitate the development of global perspectives of power and oppression. They identify nonverbal exercises, shared recognition of the difficulties of communication, role-plays, and small-group discussion as important strategies for achieving this outcome.

The impact of the informal components of the programme cannot be underestimated. The shared experiences of social and cultural activities in an atmosphere of fun and laughter literally "oiled the wheels" of the process. The Pub, the Salsa Parlour, the Taverna all contributed to cultural integration and harmony. Friendships were made, networks formed as a means of disseminating the new learning.

The learning that the students take from the seminar has been applied in their home institutions. This has led to challenges to the status quo and the modus operandi of these institutions. For example, the Greek students engaged in a dialogue with their faculty, expressing concern about their perception of an overly didactic approach to course delivery. The Irish students, on the other hand, questioned the relevance of course structures which inhibit dialogue and proceeded to create a forum to bring together students from other professional courses to address this issue.

The following represents a random sample of the comments received from the students as a result of their evaluation.

- "This week has given me a real taste of the different cultures. It has brought Europe to me and I now think I can see what role/place I have within this whole idea of Europe."
- "Our experience together has been very, very good. We have seen that we are different, diverse, but at the end we feel the same, we need the same."
- "For me personally, this week has opened a lot of issues, both on a personal and professional level. . . . It has been an inspiration to me."
- "Particularly when doing the nonverbal presentation, I felt a strong sense of teamwork and was amazed with the ease that we manage to work."
- "I have found very different mechanisms of communication."
- "I have learnt more about groupwork here in one week than five years in college."
- "I feel empowered as a result of this week's discussions."
- "I am amazed at how much I have learnt and I haven't even opened a book!"
- "I have to say that this was one of the . . . well . . . best arrangements I've ever been to."
- "In summary the power of not talking . . . I think the nonverbal presentation in conveying discrimination. As we discussed beforehand and then conveyed it nonverbally, I felt more in touch with my feelings for the person enduring discrimination."

## APPLICATION OF THE METHOD
## IN OTHER CONTEXTS

The principles and methods discussed above are transferable to many other contexts. The essential elements which make this approach so user friendly devolve around those aspects of the program which engage participants in an active manner at their own pace. The creation of a common language of communication, which is task- and process-oriented, generates the energy for the group's genesis and growth.

Beginning with the personal focus, in which participants engage with each other and the facilitators, a partnership is created which develops a shared process of ownership. The commonalities, which emerge as a result of these encounters, provide the foundation on which a scaffold for difference can be built. The construction of a forum of openness between multicultural and multilingual subgroups allows for challenge to take place and conflict to be acknowledged and resolved. This bonding further cements relationships and learning for the participants.

The power of creativity in developing and harnessing energy defies contextualisation. The central core of this method is concerned with asking the right or relevant questions. Democracy is the vital ingredient. The questions must come from and reflect the concerns of those who are oppressed. Engaging with oppression is the universalising feature of this process. To arrive at an understanding of the political dimension is vital if we are to complete the "personal is political" continuum. We believe that this is both possible and desirable because otherwise this world becomes a vast arena in which the individual is invisible and silenced. The recognition of the political nature of the process serves to provide a focus of intervention at the point where real change is possible and the balance of power can be transformed.

# REFERENCES

Ashcroft, L. (1987). "Defusing 'Empowering': The What and the Why?" *Language Arts 64*(2):145-155.

Bendor, S., Davidson, K., and Skolnik, L. (1997). "Strengths-Pathology Dissonance in Social Work Curriculum." *Journal of Teaching in Social Work 15*(1):1-2.

Boal, A. (1992). *Games for Actors and Non Actors.* London and New York: Routledge.

Coulshed, V. (1993). "Adult Learning: Implications for Teaching in Social Work Education." *British Journal of Social Work 23*(1):1-13.

Dean, G.R. (1993). "Teaching a Constructivist Approach to Clinical Practice." *Journal of Social Work Education 29*(1):1-2, 55-75.

Erdman, D.V. (Ed.) (1988). *The Complete Poetry and Prose of William Blake*. New York: Doubleday Books.

Freire, P. (1970). *The Pedagogy of the Oppressed*. New York: Herder and Herder.

Gergen, K. (1985). "The Social Constructionist Movement in Modern Psychology." *American Psychologist 40*(3):317-329.

Giddens, A. (1998). *The Third Way*. Oxford: Polity Press.

Goldstein, H. (1990). "Strength or Pathology: Ethical and Rhetorical Contrasts in Approaches to Practice." *Families in Society 71*(5):267-275.

Gurevitch, Z.D. (1989). "The Power of Not Understanding: The Meeting of Conflicting Identities." *The Journal of Applied Behavioral Science 25*(2):161-173.

Hanmer, J. and Statham, D. (1993). "Commonalities and Differences Between Women Clients and Women Social Workers." In Walmsley, J., Renolds, J., Shakespeare, P., and Woolfe, R. (Eds.), *Health, Welfare and Practice*. London: Sage Publications.

Henry, S. (1981). *Group Skills in Social Work*. Itasca, IL: Peacock Publishers.

Huff, M. and Johnson, M. (1988). "Empowering Students in a Graduate-Level Social Work Course." *Journal of Social Work Education 34*(3).

Lee, J.A.B. (1996). "The Empowerment Group Approach: An International Paradigm." In J.K. Parry (Ed.), *From Prevention to Wellness* (pp. 15-32). Binghamton, NY: The Haworth Press.

Lee, J.A.B. and Martin, R.R. (1997). "The Empowerment Group in Action." In A.S. Alissi and C.G.C. Mergins (Eds.), *Voices from the Field: Groupwork Responds* (pp. 23-42). Binghamton, NY: The Haworth Press.

Lordan, N. and Wilson, M. (1998). "Challenging Oppression through Creative Means." Paper presented at the AASWG International Conference, Miami, Florida.

Mullender, A. and Ward, D. (1991). *Self Directed Groupwork*. London: Whiting and Birch.

Real, T. (1990). "Therapeutic Use of Self in Constructionist Systemic Therapy." *Family Process 29*(3):255-272.

Saleebey, D. (1996). "The Strengths Perspective in Social Work Practice: Extensions and Cautions." *Social Work 41*(3):297-301.

Sheppard, M. (1995). "Social Work, Social Science and Practice Wisdom." *British Journal of Social Work 25*(3):265-293.

Stone, S. (1995). "Empowering Teachers, Empowering Children." *Childhood Education 71*(5):294-295.

Taylor, P. (1993). *The Texts of Paulo Freire*. Buckingham, England: The Open University Press.

Thompson, N. (1993). *Anti Discriminatory Practice*. London: Macmillan.

Toseland, R. and Rivas, R. (1998). *Groupwork Practice* (Third Edition). Boston, MA: Allyn & Bacon.

Yeats, W.B. (1933). *Vacillation in The Winding Stair*. London: Macmillan.

Chapter 2

# Seeking Alternatives to Violence: A School-Based Violence Prevention Project

Janice T. Cannon
Erin L. Gingerich

This chapter is designed to give some ideas for response options in light of the Columbine High School shootings in the suburbs of Denver and the continued levels of violence and disempowerment our youth are displaying in our communities as a whole. It is our belief that a sense of powerlessness arises when individuals and groups in our society are deemed to be valuable or invaluable. All of the value-laden processes are precursors of personal, interpersonal, communal influence, and effective social functioning. The premise of the concepts in this chapter are based in empowerment practice, that being defined as:

> a process whereby the social worker engages in a set of activi-ties with the client and the client system that aims to reduce the powerlessness that has been created by negative valuations based on membership in a stigmatized population (e.g., jocks, nerds, preppies, racial divisions). (Cruz, 1996)

These are the elements of prevention of negative self-valuation and the introduction of self-efficacy intervention. Our goal is to employ significant improvements in methodology to reduce violence among adolescents in schools and communities.

As a nation, we have watched in shock as school violence has come to the forefront of the news. As a (Colorado) community, we are numb from the most recent and largest school massacre in U.S.

history. Jefferson County, Colorado, now joins other cities and towns that rapidly went from points on a map to the center of household conversations across the country: Springfield, Edinboro, Jonesboro, West Paducah, and others. We struggle to understand these incidents of youth putting into action their internal and external conflict. And yet the shock we felt as we watched television or read the paper has begun to fade as we settle back into our comfortable and safe environments across the country. Many have become complacent and apathetic as school districts install metal detectors or hire security guards, as lobbyists and politicians argue over gun control, and we convince ourselves, "It could not happen here." Yet school violence does happen here, wherever "here" is for you, every day. Unfortunately, the glaring and extreme examples of school violence cloud our vision from seeing the violent acts of hate and intolerance that occur in every school, in every city, every day.

## *OVERVIEW OF SCHOOL VIOLENCE*

According to the Department of Education's Annual Report on School Safety (1998), nearly 10 percent of students ages twelve to nineteen report a fear of attack or harm at school. This includes violence against one's self and others. The recent school shootings have heightened the public's awareness of school violence but present a sensationalized account that overlooks the everyday threats to safety in school, ranging from bullying to physical threat and harm. Any violence in schools is too much, and the first step in addressing the problem is to get a picture of its scope:

- School-age children are nearly three times more likely to be the victim of violent crime away from school than at school.
- Threats and actual violence more often do not involve a weapon.
- Nine percent of all students surveyed report fear of attack or harm at school and nine percent also report avoiding going into one or more areas at school. It is important to note that black and Hispanic students report significantly higher levels of fear and avoidance than white students do. (Department of Education, 1998)

This statistical overview of school violence lays the groundwork for grasping the scope of school violence. Once the dimensions of a problem have been defined, one can begin to consider interventions. Multiple attempts at intervention with youth violence have been made, many with limited success because they address symptoms or outcomes of youth violence and not the root causes of the violence. Previous interventions with limited success have included: attempts to reduce access to guns by young people, increased security in schools, and imposition of harsher consequences for offenders.

It is time for an intervention to be developed that addresses the underlying feelings of worthlessness, depression, powerlessness, and isolation perpetuated by the communities in which youth are being raised that manifest themselves in acts of violence by and toward youth. Until we address the individual internal and external conflicts that all youth face, the ways in which we are all connected in society, and the fact that how we treat one another is paramount in the detection, assessment, and treatment of the violence in our society, our efforts will continue to fail.

With this in mind, the following program outline has been developed for Seeking Alternative Solutions to Violence (SASV). Its Mission Statement is as follows:

> Seeking Alternative Solutions to Violence is a student-focused and student-directed program that works to seek solutions to violence in schools. SASV works to build community, fosters responsible citizenship, and aims for collective action as tactics to reduce violence towards and by youth. Seeking solutions to and preventing violence must involve everyone in a given community; it is SASV's vision that all community members become involved in the exploration and development of solutions to violence.

## OVERVIEW OF SEEKING ALTERNATIVE SOLUTIONS TO VIOLENCE PROGRAM

SASV is a community-based empowerment project for youth who attend public and private schools. To date, there is little or no known evidence of such programs being implemented in Colorado public school systems. However, there are several similar programs in Chicago and Texas in the United States (Center for the Study and Prevention of Violence), and the Youth Challenge Project exists in western Australia (Pike, Thompson, and Thompson, 1995). SASV has been designed to accommodate the needs and desires of the particular youth and communities the program serves. A process of evaluation has been painted broadly throughout the program in order to give credence to modifications that will enhance and strengthen each component of the program. When these improvements and modifications are made, a direct correlation in the increased student participation can occur as the implementation process takes hold.

Our identified service populations are inner-city and urban youth who attend high school, public or private. The program will intertwine the participation of students, parents, citizens, school staff, public officials, and celebrity figures (often sports celebrities), as well as the community at large. Empowerment will be promoted in the community in a multidimensional manner, through the use of the voices of students as mentors. Because this program is designed to be self-supported by the school and the community, it is paramount for the residents to participate actively on all levels.

### *Relationship to Empowerment Practice*

Empowerment practice is defined as a process whereby the social worker engages in activities with the client or client system with the aim of reducing the powerlessness that has been created by negative valuations. This involves identification of power blocs that contribute to the problem as well as development and implementation of specific strategies aimed at either the reduction of the effects from indirect power blocs or the reduction of the operation of direct power blocs (Cruz, 1996).

### *SASV Program Goals*

The program goals of the Seeking Alternative Solutions to Violence (SASV) program are:

- Empowering youth and community members to operationalize their view of themselves as agents capable of achieving a solution to their individual problem(s)

- Enabling youth to view the community as a resource that has skills to assist them in their journey through life
- Assisting youth to see schools, parents, and counselors as partners in their problem-solving effort, thereby
- Encouraging youth to actualize their ability to effect changes in the power structure in their community and society at large
- Increasing community interdependence, creating also a climate for change

## *PROGRAM MODEL AND METHODOLOGIES*

The program will encompass the personal, interpersonal, and the community/political components within our society. In addition, the model surveys the individual's global sense of self-worth. In order for the empowerment process to work effectively, it will be necessary to gain the confidence of major *stakeholders* in the community. For the purposes of this project, the stakeholders are considered to be the students, parents, school staff, and citizens.

The students who participate in the program will take an active part in program design by educating other participants about their needs. It is expected that these students will utilize the tools of influence in a positive manner to increase the levels of participation among their peer groups. The role of parents often times has been limited to participation in the planning process only. This, in effect, has rendered parents ineffective. SASV considers parents a vital program partner. The role of school staff is also essential in any intervention with youth. School faculty will assist in encouraging the participation of students and parents. Faculty will have the opportunity to work with youth using nontraditional methods that will influence their role in the academic setting. The role and participation of citizens and the community at large are viewed as an integral component (Kieffer, 1984). Focusing on citizen participation as a form of empowerment will provide outreach and intervention opportunities. The following areas will be considered:

- Behavior and participation can be monitored and directly measured.
- Participation on various levels (individual, organizational, community) will be monitored.

Research in the area of participation in community-based organizations in three cities has found both community-focused cognition and behavior and aggregated community-level variables to be the best predictors of participation (Kieffer, 1984).

### Intervention Strategies

In relation to intervention strategies, all interventions are designed to reflect human and cultural diversity. With a focus on cultural diversity, it is important to note that there are issues (e.g., HIV-transmission prevention, pregnancy prevention) that present challenges to traditional methods of problem resolution. These issues may require a number of specialized interventions. By being cognizant of these factors, interventions can be designed to address various gender, ethnic, age, cultural, and other group differences. The interventions proposed for the SASV program are focused on individuals, groups, schools, and communities.

With regard to groups, a primary goal is to empower the members to take control, with provisional support for participants. Research notes that self-help individual and group efforts are perhaps the most salient of tools to assist people in the empowerment process. In addition, groups have had a lasting effect in organizational and institutional settings in bringing about change and empowerment.

### Project Activities

A set of project activities, in sequence, has been identified. They are as follows:

1. In each community, stakeholders will be identified. Individuals will be selected based on their credibility in the particular community in which SASV is based. A communication meeting will be held in order to engage the community leaders' support.
2. Communication Training Sessions will be held and will include the following components:
   • Short pretraining seminar to assess the attitudes and beliefs of the volunteers/participants
   • Interactive training designed to encourage vertical and horizontal dialogue between students, parents, teachers, and community members

The training will cover:
- Parenting strategies
- Problem-solving strategies
- Effective communication
- Role-playing
3. Once the stakeholders are trained, relationships will become more formalized with the host school (whether elementary, middle, or high school). A "Training the Trainers" curriculum will also be developed from the information and experiences of the stakeholders.
4. Alternative host sites may be used; however, the school tends to be a neutral site with a number of on-site activities and facilities—gymnasiums, kitchens, auditoriums, libraries, computers, swimming pools, etc. The stakeholders will construct a school-based intervention that focuses on meeting the needs of their immediate community.

## *Program Components*

The community stakeholders will select the components of the program, with consultation from SASV staff. The components may include but are not limited to:
1. Mentoring programs
2. Group sessions and class sessions that cover the following material:
   - Self-efficacy
   - Drug and alcohol use and abuse
   - Anger management
   - Time management
   - Cognition
   - Health and wellness
   - Antiviolence behaviors
3. One-on-one therapeutic sessions
4. Cooking classes
5. Physical education
6. Theater and music
7. Career counseling
8. Tutorial programs
9. Community activism
10. Cultural tolerance programs

Any combination of the above may be incorporated as part of a specific community's program design. Ideally, the more structured programs will be held three days per week, leaving the other days free for both recreational activities and community activism.

## PROJECTED OUTCOMES

Referring to the program goals and the generalized goal of SASV to reduce powerlessness, prevent negative self-valuation, provide self-efficacy intervention, and end violence against and by youth, the following projected program outcomes may be anticipated:

- Increased sense of self-worth among youth, their schools, and within their communities
- Increased sense of belonging on the part of youth
- Decreased number of physical altercations
- Improved attitudes toward school and faculty members on the part of students
- Improved cooperation among school staff, including faculty members, students, parents, and the community at large
- Increased use of community resources
- Increased level of political activism

Monitoring and evaluation strategies will need to be found or created and put in place so that the ongoing efficiency, effectiveness, and efficacy of the Seeking Alternative Solutions to Violence Program may be measured, the program modified according to feedback, and the results shared with others around the country and around the world who seek ways of eliminating all forms of violence.

The program model, intervention strategies, project activities, and program components outlined above, employed through empowerment-based practice and school-based actions in conjunction with community involvement, may be put in place to reduce violence by and toward youth.

# REFERENCES

Center for the Study and Prevention of Violence, University of Colorado. <http://www.colorado.edu/cspv/blueprints/model/>.

Corvo, K.N. (1997). Community-based youth violence prevention: A framework for planners and funders. *Youth and Society* 28(3):291-315.

Cruz, V. (1996). Class lecture: Introduction to social work practice. Metropolitan State College, Denver, Colorado.

Department of Education (1998). *Annual report on school safety.* Washington, DC: United States Government Printing Office.

Kieffer, C. (1984). Citizen empowerment: A developmental perspective. *Prevention in Human Services* 3(Winter/Spring):9-36.

Pike, L.T., Thompson, A.L., Thompson, L.J. (1995). The youth challenge project: Models, measurement and mentors. *Issues in Educational Research* 5(1):53-70.

Chapter 3

# Social Work Empowerment Agenda and Group Work: A Workshop

Jean F. East
Susan S. Manning
Ruth J. Parsons

## *OVERVIEW*

The closing plenary session of the Twenty-First Annual AASWG Symposium on Social Work with Groups was a presentation on group work and empowerment as a practice theory and intervention. The session involved participants in responding to key questions about group work and empowerment principles. The workshop tied together many of the themes of the symposium by emphasizing that group work is a central method of empowerment-based practice. This article is a summary of that workshop.

## *PART I: EMPOWERMENT*

The first part of the plenary session was a presentation of the historical, theoretical, and research foundations of empowerment practice. The works of numerous authors were cited. (See Breton, 1994; Cox, 1988; Cox and Parsons, 1994; East, 1999a; Gutierrez, 1990 and 1991; Gutierrez and Nurius, 1994; Gutierrez, Parsons, and Cox, 1998; Lee, 1994; Manning, 1999; Miley, O'Melia, and DuBois, 1998; Mondros and Wilson, 1994; Pinderhughes, 1983; Shera and Wells, 1999; Simon, 1994; Whitmore, 1991.)

For the purpose of this summary, a few key themes from the presentation were outlined. First is empowerment, which Torre (1985) defined as *"a process through which individuals and groups become strong enough to participate within, share in the control of, and influence events and institutions affecting their lives; and that, in part, empowerment necessitates that people gain particular skills, knowledge, and sufficient power to influence their lives and the lives of those they care about"* (1985, pp. 42-43).

Second, the components of empowerment practice were outlined. These have been included as constituent elements of empowerment-oriented practice by a number of authors. (See Breton, 1994; Cox and Parsons, 1994; East, 1999b, 2000; Gutierrez, Parsons, and Cox, 1998). The three elements of empowerment practice presented included:

1. *Personal: attitudes, values, and beliefs.* The personal dimension contains psychological components developed through the empowerment process, including self-efficacy (Bandura, 1977; Tipton and Worthington, 1984), perceived control/self-esteem (Paulhus and Cristie, 1981), and an internal locus of control (Rotter, 1966; Simmons and Parsons, 1983a). Personal empowerment may also include a reduction of alienation and learned helplessness (Seligman, 1972; Seeman, 1975), and perceived sociopolitical control (Zimmerman and Zanhiser, 1991).

2. *Interpersonal: knowledge, skills, networks.* The interpersonal dimension of empowerment involves learning to negotiate one's immediate social world. It includes an ability to access environmental structures and includes knowledge and skills needed to manage and resolve one's problems, including communication skills, assertiveness skills, and the ability to broker resources and advocate for one's self and for others (Cox, 1988; Cox and Parsons, 1994; Gutierrez, 1990; Simmons and Parsons, 1983a; Zimmerman, 1990b, 1995, 2000). Social support is a part of the interaction dimension and is defined as the emotional and instrumental assistance obtained from people who comprise the individual's social network (Berkman, 1984).

3. *Socio/political: individual and collective action.* The third dimension involves participating in the larger community and taking action on one's own behalf and/or on behalf of others and includes: participation in community activities, voting, joining organizations, and participating in social action (Cox, 1988; Cox

and Parsons, 1994; Florin and Wandersman, 1990; Kieffer, 1981; Solomon, 1976; Zimmerman, 1990a; Zimmerman and Rappaport, 1988; Zimmerman and Zanhiser, 1991).

The third theme of the presentation was the link between empowerment and social group work. Ruby Pernell was acknowledged for her initial work in this area and her claim that "groups are a natural context for efforts toward empowerment" (Pernell, 1986, p. 114). Pernell concluded her article by saying:

> Our summary is in definitions. . . . Power: The ability to act or perform effectively. . . . Empowerment: The capacity to influence the forces which affect one's life space for one's own and other's benefit. . . . Social Group Work: A method with the potential for achieving the above. (1986, p. 117)

In summary, empowerment is about increasing the power of individuals and groups of individuals. There are three elements that are part of the empowerment process and can make up empowerment practice: personal, interpersonal, and political. Finally, social group work is a natural context for empowerment practice models.

## PART II:
## GROUP WORK AND EMPOWERMENT
## SUPPORTS AND CHALLENGES

Following the presentation of the above material, the second part of the workshop was an interactive small-group process. The goal of this process was for participants to relate empowerment principles to different types of groups.

First, people were asked to identify the supports and challenges to empowerment for each of the three dimensions, personal, interpersonal, and community/political. They were asked to think of these dimensions according to the type of group with which they functioned as a social work practitioner. They recorded this information on work sheets individually. Next, the workshop participants were asked to self-select into types of groups. Three small groups formed: (1) Therapeutic, (2) Social Action, and (3) Task Groups.

Through interaction, each group was asked to identify one to three challenges and one to three supports for promoting an empowerment agenda in their work with groups. This information was then reported back to the group as a whole. As each group reported, the information was interpreted by the presenters in terms of the empowerment literature. A synthesis of the small groups' ideas and the presenters interpretation is presented below. The interpretation of the authors is in sans serif type.

### *Therapeutic Groups*

As identified by workshop participants, there are both supports and challenges in carrying out an empowerment perspective in therapeutic groups.

The *supports* of the development of *personal and interpersonal* empowerment processes include:

- The feeling of being cared about and caring for others; opportunity for respect from others
- The opportunity to break isolation, to experience mutual aid and peer support
- Cohesiveness in a group
- Acknowledgement of the rights and responsibilities of members
- Giving and receiving feedback

Therapeutic group work seems to support both the personal and interpersonal dimensions of empowerment as identified in the research and literature. Caring and respect conveyed by others helps to reduce self-blame and enhances a feeling of self-efficacy (Gutierrez, 1989). Rights and responsibilities promote self-determination. Belonging to a community or group reduces isolation, an important goal of both group work and empowerment. The interaction inherent in a group creates opportunities for participation, contribution and action, and taking the responsibility to help others, all of which help people feel more empowered (Manning, Zibalese-Crawford, and Downey, 1994).

The *challenges* to developing the personal and interpersonal components of empowerment practice in therapeutic groups include:

- Not enough time, within agency restrictions, to work with individuals in an empowering way
- Professional socialization, role, and work overload
- Environmental issues and resources (e.g., facility, materials, transportation, access to group)
- Preexisting stereotypes (the stigma that exists about consumer ability to be empowered)

The current realities of group work, particularly in agency settings, also create challenges to implementing an empowerment perspective. As Kieffer (1984) found, empowerment is a developmental process that takes time, and agency practice may limit this time. In addition, professional socialization can get in the way of the empowerment agenda. As Breton (1994) stated, "practitioners have to abandon the expert role" (p. 29). The worker as the expert and the client as needing professional expertise can be part of a social work professional culture and North American culture (Rappaport, 1985). An empowerment philosophy calls for valuing of client competency and "requires developing peer relationships and collaborative strategies" (Breton, 1994, p. 29). Finally, as Lee noted, "empowerment groups emerge from empowering agencies" (1994, p. 251). The agency commitment to an empowerment philosophy of services may influence how clients are perceived.

In the *political* dimension of empowerment practice, the *supports and challenges* for therapeutic groups include:

Supports:

- A vision about empowerment that can extend into the community
- Identification with the larger community that promotes civic responsibility
- Institutional openness, which can bring a forum for advocacy

Challenges:

- Lack of institutional openness or respect for empowerment that restricts advocacy
- Hierarchy of power
- Empowerment can be viewed as a threat to agency

The therapeutic group can be an avenue to the political dimension of empowerment for clients/consumers (Lee, 1994). Looking to the community and facilitating social action can provide a connection for individuals beyond the therapeutic group (Breton, 1994). The opportunity to have a forum for dialogue about issues helps to develop critical thinking and problem-solving skills. The challenges of implementing an empowerment agenda often represent issues of structure and philosophy within agencies. For an empowerment agenda to develop, structures must be put in place that provide opportunities for client/consumer participation in the decisions that affect them (Maton and Salem, 1995).

## *Social Action Groups*

Workshop participants in the social action group reported *supports and challenges* to empowerment practice in general, not as related to the specific dimensions of empowerment.

Supports included:

- Creation of a supportive environment
- Issues identified for action
- Resources that are identified, such as community support systems, leaders, money and other material resources
- Commitment and wide community participation
- Knowledge of the change process

Many of the above supports in social action groups relate to the knowledge and skill-building components of empowerment. Social action groups, by their nature, prompt members to identify desired changes, develop political savvy, develop resources, and learn new skills to negotiate the political process (East, 2000). Empowerment is a natural outcome of these activities. In the social action process, members find value in their contributions and abilities, which contributes to a sense of self-determination and control. Participation and knowledge of the change process are also important components of an empowerment process (Parsons, East, and Boesen, 1994).

Challenges included:

- Lack of resources, money
- Resistance from within social work or the community

- Conflicts of interest, political ideologies of individuals and group (unwilling to compromise)
- Lack of awareness of broader issues in the community, misinformation
- Difficulty in developing coalitions autonomously (without loss of identity or compromising of self)
- Gender bias
- Culture of group (e.g., not speaking up, relationship to authority, resistance to process)

The challenges to an empowerment model in social action groups can be many. Lack of resources and money are critical issues as advocacy groups struggle for their existence (Mondros and Wilson, 1994). In social action work, the resources of knowledge and people become the means for empowerment. Therefore, workers must make special efforts to seek out good information, build coalitions, respect diversity, encourage women and people of color to develop leadership skills, and support the skill building necessary to develop empowerment in members. Social action from an empowerment perspective requires strong collaboration and consensus-building skills on the part of the worker and eventually on the part of group members (Longres and McLeod, 1980).

## *Task Groups*

The Task Group participants reported their results as general challenges to an empowerment model. These challenges were identified through the process of discussing a real-life problem from a task group.

Challenges included:

- Definition of the task, definition of purpose, and acceptance of the task with a diversity of perceptions
- Worker: Creating social relationships and climate, cohesion, conflict mediation; valuing all contributions
- Setting up rules for making decisions, consistent searching for consensus, learning the problem-solving process
- Providing a voice for everyone; satisfying solutions on the individual and collective level

- Giving people real responsibilities with accountability
- Time: how workers use the time we have; limits on how we use it
- Relating to external factors
- Evaluation
- Creating a sense of hope from the worker

Task groups often take place within an agency or organization; thus, the dilemmas are related to empowerment within organizations. Agency culture and social climate within an organization, or for a particular task group, reflect values and beliefs that can facilitate or act as a barrier to empowerment. Maton and Salem (1995) identified four factors that nurture empowering settings in organizations: (1) an inspiring, strengths-based belief system focused beyond self, (2) an accessible role structure, (3) an inspiring, shared leadership, and (4) a peer-based support system that creates a sense of community. If these four factors are present in an organization, many barriers to empowerment can be addressed. Norms for group processes, such as participatory decision making, can be nurtured. Peer support for diversity of perspectives can be fostered while encouraging group members to focus beyond themselves to a larger mission. Ultimately, inspiring and shared leadership can lead to meaningful participation in task groups which promotes empowerment at all levels.

## CONCLUSION

This conclusion is a combination of some final thoughts and comments by the presenters and an analysis of key themes as they emerged both from the literature review and from the workshop participant responses.

### Consciousness

A change in consciousness is necessary to practice from an empowerment perspective (Manning, Parsons, and Silver, 1997). Attitudes must be developed that reinforce client potential and re-distribute power. This can feel risky, to both individual practitioners and to agencies. The redistribution of power from traditional "expert" to that of collaboration and partnership can change the nature of the helping relationship to "doing with" rather than "doing for." This is not always easy, especially in some practice settings, and takes ongoing critical awareness on the part of the social worker (Breton, 1994).

## Connectedness Over Time

Increased power and empowerment for individuals or groups in the three dimensions—personal, interpersonal, and political—is a developmental process (Kieffer, 1984). It takes time and it is often "messy," in that it is not a linear process. This can be a challenge for social workers in any type of group setting. Workers must be prepared to structure extra time for the processes necessary to share power, prepare members to take responsibilities, have "failures" along the way, and build a sense of connectedness that promotes multiple levels of action.

## A Learning Environment

An important part of an empowerment intervention model is the creation of a learning environment that promotes empowerment (Manning, Parsons, and Silver, 1997). Many of the challenges identified by workshop participants related to the external environment of group work, including agencies, policy, and community barriers. In order to change these structures, both clients and workers can take the opportunity of the group to critically analyze these structures and develop subsequent strategies for intervention and change (Lee, 1994). Such changes may mean including consumers in the governance structures, promoting leadership roles for staff and clients, using participatory and action research models to evaluate programs, and creating agency cultures that promote ongoing learning and growth for both individuals and organizations (Gutierrez and Nurius, 1994).

## Collectivity: Groups and Community

An empowerment model of practice requires that social work interventions promote collectivity for groups of people that are disadvantaged and lacking power (Breton, 1994). Working with people in groups and in community settings can be a natural way to accomplish this. Whether the group is a therapeutic, social action, or task group, the group can become an avenue to a sense of belonging, education, critical analysis of the environment, participation in decisions at many levels, and change at the personal, interpersonal, and political levels. As Pernell (1986) stated, the group is an opportunity system.

## Hope

An empowerment model, by its very nature, conveys a sense of hope. It includes a focus on the self-esteem and self-confidence of the individual, on skill building and the development of critical thinking, and on the integration of the individual with a collective. There is also an opportunity for choice and responsibility, the expectation of contribution, and an emphasis on taking action. This combination provides a framework for groups, whether they be groups of client/consumers or groups of service providers, to become a significant part of the empowerment agenda.

As the participants in this symposium demonstrated by their input, there are both sources of support and challenges in integrating an empowerment practice model with social group work practice. With the right conditions, however, it can be accomplished.

## REFERENCES

Bandura, A. (1977). Self-efficacy: Towards a unifying theory of behavioral change. *Psychological Review 84*:191-215.

Berkman, L. (1984). Assessing the physical health effects of social networkers and social support. In D. Breslow, J.E. Field, and L.B. Lave (Eds.), *Annual review of public health*, vol. 5 (pp. 27-43). Palo Alto, CA: Annual Review.

Breton, M. (1994). On the meaning of empowerment and empowerment oriented social work practice. *Social Work with Groups 17*(3):23-38.

Cox, E. (1988). Empowerment of the low income elderly through group work. *Social Work with Groups 11*(3/4):111-125.

Cox, E. and Parsons, R.J. (1994). *Empowerment-oriented social work practice with the elderly*. Pacific Grove, CA: Brooks/Cole.

East, J. (1999a). An empowerment practice model for low-income women. In W. Shera and L. Wells (Eds.), *Empowerment practice in social work: Developing richer conceptual foundations* (pp. 142-158). Toronto: Canadian Scholars Press.

East, J. (1999b). Hidden barriers to success for women in welfare reform. *Families in Society: The Journal of Contemporary Human Services* (May-June):295-304.

East, J. (2000). Empowerment through welfare-rights organizing: A feminist perspective. *Afflia 15*(2):311-328.

Florin, P. and Wandersman, A. (1990). An introduction to citizen participation, voluntary organizations and community development: Insights for empowerment through research. *American Journal of Community Psychology 18*(1):41-54.

Gutierrez, L.M. (1989). Empowerment in social work practice: Considerations for practice and education. Paper presented to the Council on Social Work Education, Annual Program Meeting, Chicago, IL.

Gutierrez, L.M. (1990). Working with women of color: An empowerment perspective. *Social Work 35*(2):16-32.

Gutierrez, L.M. (1991). Developing methods to empower Latinos. *Social Work with Groups 14*(2):23.

Gutierrez, L.M., DeLois, K.A., and GlenMaye, L. (1994). Understanding empowerment-based practice: Building on practitioner-based knowledge. *Families in Society 76*(9):534-542.

Gutierrez, L.M. and Nurius, P. (Eds.) (1994). *Education and research for empowerment practice.* Seattle, WA: Center for Policy and Practice Research, School of Social Work, University of Washington.

Gutierrez, L.M., Parsons, R.J., and Cox, E.O. (Eds.) (1998). *Empowerment in social work practice: A sourcebook.* Pacific Grove, CA: Brooks/Cole.

Hirayama, H. and Hirayama, K. (1986). Empowerment through group participation: Process and goal. In Parnes, M. (Ed.), *Innovations in social group work: Feedback from practice to theory* (pp. 119-131). Binghamton, NY: The Haworth Press, Inc.

Kieffer, C. (1981). The emergence of empowerment: The development of participatory competence among individuals in citizen organizations. Unpublished doctoral dissertation, University of Michigan.

Kieffer, C. (1984). Citizen empowerment: A developmental perspective. *Prevention in Human Services 3* (Winter/Spring):9-36.

Lee, J.A.B. (1994). *The empowerment approach to social work practice.* New York: Columbia University Press.

Longres, J.F. and McLeod, E. (1980). Consciousness-raising and social work practice. *Social Casework: The Journal of Contemporary Social Work 61*(5):267-276.

Manning, S. (1999). Building an empowerment model of practice through the voices of people with serious psychiatric disability. In Shera, W. and Wells, L. (Eds.), *Empowerment practice in social work: Developing richer conceptual foundations* (pp. 102-118). Toronto: Canadian Scholars' Press.

Manning, S., Parsons, R., and Silver, S. (1997). An empowerment model for persons with serious psychiatric disability. Denver, CO: University of Denver Graduate School of Social Work.

Manning, S., Zibalese-Crawford, M., and Downey, E. (1994). Colorado mental health consumer family development project. Program evaluation report. Denver, CO: Colorado Division of Mental Health.

Maton, K. and Salem, D. (1995). Organizational characteristics of empowering community settings: A multiple case study approach. *American Journal of Community Psychology 23*(50):631-656.

Miley, K.K., O'Melia, M., and DuBois, B. (1998). *Generalist social work practice: An empowerment approach*. Boston, MA: Allyn & Bacon.

Mondros, J.B. and Wilson, S.M. (1994). *Organizing for power and empowerment*. New York: Columbia University Press.

Parsons, R.J. and Cox, E.O. (1992). Empowerment through group collectivity: An old approach to building community. Presentation at the Council on Social Work Education Annual Program Meeting, Kansas City, KS.

Parsons, R.J., East, J.F., and Boesen, M.B. (1994). Empowerment: A case study with AFDC women. In Gutierrez, L.M. and Nurius, P. (Eds.), *Education and research for empowerment practice* (pp. 259-272). Seattle, WA: Center for Policy and Practice Research, School of Social Work, University of Washington.

Paulhus, D. and Christie, R. (1981). Spheres of control: An interactionist approach to assessment of perceived control. In Lefcourt, H.M. (Ed.) *Research with the focus of control construct*, vol. 1, Assessment Methods (pp. 253-265). New York: Academic Press.

Pernell, R. (1986). Empowerment and social group work. In Parnes, M. (Ed.), *Innovations in social group work: Feedback from practice to theory*. Binghamton, NY: The Haworth Press, Inc.

Pinderhughes, E. (1983). Empowerment for our clients and for ourselves. *Social Casework 64*(6):331-338.

Rappaport, J. (1985). The power of empowerment language. *Social Policy 16*(2):15-21.

Revicki, D.A. and Mitchell, J. (1986). Social support factor in the elderly. *Research in Aging 8*(2):232-258.

Rotter, J. (1966). Generalized expectancies for internal vs. external control reinforcement. *Psychological Monographs 80*(609):1014-1053.

Seeman, M. (1975). Alienation studies. In Coleman, J. and Smelser, N. (Eds) *Annual review of sociology*, vol. 1 (pp. 91-123). Palo Alto, CA: Annual Reviews, Inc.

Seligman, M. (1972). *Helplessness: On depression development and death*. San Francisco, CA: Freeman.

Shera, W. and Wells, L. (Eds.) (1999). *Empowerment practice in social work: Developing richer conceptual foundations*. Toronto: Canadian Scholars' Press.

Simmons, C. and Parsons, R.J. (1983). Empowerment for role alternatives in adolescence. *Adolescence 27*(69):196-198.

Simon, B.L. (1994). *Empowerment traditions: History of empowerment in social work*. New York: Columbia University Press.

Solomon, B. (1976). *Black empowerment: Social work in oppressed communities*. New York: Columbia University Press.

Tipton, R.M. and Worthington, E.L. (1984). The measurement of generalized self-efficacy: A study of construct validity. *Journal of Personality Assessment 48*(5): 545-549.

Torre, D. (1985). *Empowerment: Structured conceptualization and instrument development.* Unpublished doctoral dissertation, Cornell University, New York.

Whitmore, E. (1991). Evaluation and empowerment: It's the process that counts. *Networking Bulletin* 2(2):1-7.

Zimmerman, M.A. (1990a). Toward a theory of learned hopefulness: A structural model analysis of participation and empowerment. *Journal of Research in Personality* 24(1):71-86.

Zimmerman, M.A. (1990b) Taking aim on empowerment research: On the distinction between individual and psychological concepts. *American Journal of Community Psychology* 18(1):169-177.

Zimmerman, M. (1995). Psychological empowerment: Issues and illustrations. *American Journal of Community Psychology* 23(5):581-599.

Zimmerman, M.A. (2000). Empowerment theory: psychological, organizational, and community levels of analysis. In Rappaport, J. and Seidmen, E. (Eds.), *Handbook of Community Psychology* (pp. 43-64). New York: Plenum Press.

Zimmerman, M.A. and Rappaport, J. (1988). Citizen participation, perceived control and psychological empowerment. *American Journal of Community Psychology* 16(5):725-750.

Zimmerman, M.A. and Zanhiser, J. (1991). Refinements of sphere-specific measures of perceived control: Development of a sociopolitical control scale. *Journal of Community Psychology* 19(4):189-204.

*PART II:*
*SYMPOSIUM PRESENTATIONS*

Chapter 4

# Narrative Social Work with Groups: Just in Time

Paul Abels
Sonia Leib Abels

We are living in a postmodern, reconstructive era in which the profession's helping processes need to be assessed in relationship to technological advances, which have a strong impact on the nature of human connection and self-image. We see two changes as particularly important: the first, the changing perceptions of time, exemplified by the Web and e-mail; and the second, advances in knowledge of genetics and learned behavior, and the degree to which each shapes human development. These developments are changing the nature of social interactions and will increasingly create major social concerns for clients and helpers as the social context begins to impact traditional patterns of interaction. Both of these developments are closely related to class and inequality issues. We have begun to see the nature of interaction change as face-to-face contacts diminish and "chat" rooms increase.

## *THE NARRATIVE PRACTICE APPROACH*

In the search for more effective means of helping people with both the social and emotional concerns that connect their everyday lives to these changes, we have found that narrative practice offers a social work approach which supports people's search for meaning and desired futures. In the face of media hype, which also promotes the idea that their lives are increasingly genetically determined, narrative emphasizes the importance of context and of society's major shaping role. The stories that we have come to believe about ourselves structure our lives, and that basic idea is the cornerstone of a helping approach that has become a major force in work with families and an influence in practice at all levels.

Narrative practice is efficacious in aiding and assisting people to reconstruct a culture that values human relations. Like social work, its theoretical and philosophical landscape emphasizes internal and external mutual aid, connectedness, and cultural context as a determinant of both the stress and supports society offers the social self. It negates the belief that all problems are within the person. Congruent with the requirements for a contemporary mode of practice, narrative's social-context orientation makes it responsive to the recent changes in the meaning of time, the impact of both heredity and of lived experiences, as well as the significance of context in shaping a person's narratives, and it is keenly sensitive to the importance of power in controlling thought and action.

## THE NEED TO QUESTION
## PRIVILEGED POSITIONS

Social work with groups, the profession's central and most important approach to helping, may not be meeting the challenges of our day. Some social workers speak of the need for more research and grounded theory, casting intellectual doubt on the sacred cows of systems and ecological approaches, and our willingness to privilege certain helping modes over others without supportive data (Wakefield, 1996).

Postmodernism, spurred by the civil rights, gay, and feminist movements, has increased skepticism about accepting traditional historical truths in science, history, literature, and the social sciences. We do not hold the extreme view that there is no truth, nor good practice models, but, rather, that no approach should be privileged or hold hegemony over other forms of practice without examination of its value.

Ivan Illich's call for "convivial tools" (p. 3) and Michel Foucault's discussions of "subjugated knowledge" (p. 82) call attention to the damage done when influential groups control knowledge. "Knowledge is power" is the rallying call, and knowledge power should be available to all (Illich, 1973; Foucault, 1980). Fanon, working as a psychiatrist, made similar observations about privileged approaches in therapy and education, and their control by the elite through jargon, and the mystique of the expert, and disregard for the oppressed, particularly the colonized population he was working with. Foucault recognized that many of the developments in institutions of society were developed as mechanisms of control by those in power to insure their being able to maintain their privileged places in society. Their ability to label certain groups was one way to oversee their maintenance of control. The institutionalized efforts to prevent certain groups from being able to read, and the use of special languages, are cases in point.

## OUR CHANGING PERCEPTION OF TIME

Technological advances, the Web, and MTV programs speed up people's views of time and foment the desire for "quick time" change. An article in *The New York Times* on the use of stories by business noted, "People are time starved, they're drained, their attention span is short, they're full of stress" (Quines, 1991, p. 4). James Gleick's book, *Faster,* a best-seller, documents people's lack of willingness to "spend time" on reflection—everything must be done quickly; people must save time, not waste time. One student, working with a family preservation group, referred by the courts, told me that the members felt they were "putting in time," i.e., counting the number of sessions they still had to go. This may be true for many of the groups we work with. Time has become an important factor in social work. Welfare recipients have been given a "time" by which they need to find a job or be put off welfare. Foster care parents and institutions are told to put "problem children" on "time out," usually isolated. And clients who are not "on time" usually are assessed as resistant. Think about your own decisions about how to "use" your time today and the choices made prior to attending this conference.

This "time warp" has created a "mind warp" as far as people's concern with wasting time. There is guilt in "spending" time with others unless there is something to be gained by it. There is no need to invest oneself in the anonymous people in Internet chat rooms; you can just evaluate their suggestions as to what stocks to buy. Neither attachments nor commitments are necessary, and one can even get an emotional "quick fix" from another "chatter" or, for a slight charge, turn to one of over a hundred mental health "experts" who advertise on the Web.

## EFFECTS OF SOCIETAL CHANGE
## ON GROUP PRACTICE

We, the authors, question whether our practice has kept pace with the changes in society. Do we know how group dynamics, or phase theory, has been influenced by the nature of "quick time," or how the media impacts group member actions and our practice? For example, working with an oncology group, the worker had not realized how much media sexism characterized some physicians' treatment in breast reconstruction until she was asked by a physician to view some pictures in *Playboy* and select the breast she wanted. Even though other group members had gone through similar experiences, none of them had brought it to the group. Nor did the worker bring up the subject, as it was taking place outside of the group (Maram, 1998). This reflects some of the need to expand our efforts in increasing the members' recognition of the contextual nature of their situations. We have not fully recognized nor utilized the meanings that members assign to the interrelations among the members, and the links between the internal processes in the group and the members external experiences.

As the group members are working on how they want their lives to move, and how they can help each other achieve their ends, the group as a group can work on how the group's landscape can move. How they can impact society's (the physicians') treatment of women? Can the group meet with or send a letter to the physician? How can they impact the social milieu by social action? The narrative practitioner would aid the physician and the group to help each other and other women deal with such derisive actions and penetrate more deeply the societal forces related to breast cancer.

Our practice has expanded into "new" settings and "new" client groups, but the practice itself does not appear new. Social work's ability to help people is a result of the profession's increasing use of groups, which ironically parallels the diminishment of courses in group work, more often cavalierly referred to in generalist courses, usually as "group therapy" rather than social group work, or presented as six preplanned sessions of family life education, teaching childcare, and parenting skills.

How has the practice of group work changed, improved, modified, or expanded its theoretical base or its practice methodology? What new theoretical perspectives have augmented group work practice? Changing societal contexts and questionable successes call for modified helping paradigms. The exposition of systems and ecological ideas alerted us to holistic thinking, but neither concept provides interventions. Nor has group work provided direction on how to deal with ways to change the social forces that impact our clients. Narrative practice helps our clients see how those forces have recruited them into certain beliefs about themselves. We are still preparing social workers to be generalists, a rarified concept with little substance.

## NARRATIVE PRACTICE AS RESPONSE TO SOCIETAL CHANGE

We are not alone in our concerns about serving people as adequately as we would like; all of the helping professions face similar concerns. However, for a profession which sees itself as more than therapy, it behooves us to expand our practice. Narrative practice is a natural approach. It recognizes that people create stories of their lives by organizing their experiences into some cohesive whole. Thus stories shape people's lives. Bruner (1991) notes that "we organize our experience and our memory of human happenings mainly in the form of narratives, stories, excuses, myths, reasons for doing and not doing" (p. 4). Narrative practice examines how these stories help and hinder us from finding the meaning we seek in our lives. Narrative practice influences understanding, relationships, and behaviors at all structural levels: individual, family, group, and organization. The emphasis on family stories is important at a time when people are increasingly aware of how genetics is shaping their behavior. Life stories indicate that families are also shaped by life experience, not only genetic mandates. While the teenage son might resemble his father physically, their life stories are very different, shaped by the times and the opportunities each is born into.

Richard Lewontin, a geneticist, makes a similar point, as Weinar notes: "The reason he is eating this particular lunch is not in his genes, Lewontin says, holding it up. 'I'm eating it because of my social position in this culture and what's available and what lunch I got to eat when I was a kid.' This is a lunch that is typical of his time and his place and his culture but not of his species. 'Most people in the world don't eat pizza and cookies'" (Weiner, 1999, p. 218). At least not yet.

While we have discussed narrative practice more fully elsewhere (Abels and Abels, 1998), a brief review is necessary. The stories that give meaning to people's lives are most often positive, but they can also be destructive. They may be narratives of oppression, submission, and control by powerful others. Narrative practice helps people reauthor their narratives as a means of gaining control of their lives. It is future oriented, going beyond the therapeutic, incorporating ideas of social change, individual resistance, and protest as parallel processes in working with both individuals and groups. It is a particularly valuable process for a profession committed to individual and social change, and social justice. The worker and group members examine where problem-oriented stories may have come from. Members make connections and, through mutual aid, search for means to gain some control over the forces that shaped their negative narratives. Salman Rushdie said:

> Those who do not have power over the story that dominates their lives, power to retell it, rethink it, deconstruct it, and joke about it, and change it as times change, truly are powerless, because they cannot think new thoughts. (Rushdie, 1995)

The philosophical underpinnings of narrative practice reflect the values of social work: treating people with respect and dignity, not being the expert, and recognizing the importance of the relationship between the worker and those served. (Research indicates that client perceptions of the client/worker relationship are a major aspect of helping's success or failure). Narrative practice differs from traditional approaches, both theoretically and technically, in a number of ways. The worker's interaction with the group members is more like a "conversation with a purpose" than an interview. There is no attempt to make assessments, which often are the worker's preferred story rather than the members. In narrative practice, the worker focuses on what is important to the clients, not on what the worker believes is important. There is careful attention to the clients' stories without imposing the worker's story into it. Most exceptional, however, is the concept of externalizing the problem. This externalizing process permits clients to recognize that they are not always to blame for the conditions that brought them for help. Internalization leads people to believe that there is something wrong with them, that they are worthless. Narrative practice helps women on welfare, for example, to understand that, despite the verbal attacks and shame imposed on them, social conditions may be at fault, and that they have shown amazing strength in bringing up their children. This provides grounds for a new story in their lives. Asking teenage girls with eating disorders, "Where did the idea come from that it is important to be thin?" helps them understand the external pressures at work by peers, by the media, by advertising. Asking "Why does anorexia want to kill you?" may help them see anorexia as an enemy, something out there, objectified, that can be dealt with. Instead of the person being objectified, the problem is objectified. Assisting them in making contact with other teens, those who have been able to defeat anorexia and those currently dealing with it, increases the power that narrative has to help. The worker is not the only, and perhaps not even the major, helper.

## SPECIFIC NARRATIVE STRATEGIES AND RESULTS

Dean (1998) itemizes several strategies for using narratives in groups. She notes that the telling and the responses from others can be very helpful. Exchanging and expanding stories by the members involves interaction and building on each others' stories. She discusses externalizing problems and the creation of preferred accounts. One of the strategies that she uses is changing blaming stories by challenging the assumptions behind them (pp. 31-35).

Narrative practice theory is based on the idea that clients are their own best consultants, and when working in cross-cultural situations the client can help the worker and other members understand what needs to be understood. When a worker is involved with a group that differs culturally or racially, for example, from the worker, she or he might ask the members if they would like to bring in another person who might help the worker better understand their perspectives and/or make them feel more comfortable.

The use of a reflective team is another way to help an individual or the group, and serves to minimize the view of the worker as an expert. The members listening to the reflective team can then question why and what the team saw, becoming both questioners and audience to their own change. While people external to the clients' situation often make up the reflective team, it is possible to use part of the group to observe the remainder of the group's process and to comment. Both groups then discuss the responses.

Narrative practice helps clients examine how the problem not only controls the life of the clients but also influences others such as family, school, and friends. By mapping the problem, the worker begins to see and to show others how the problem impacts not only the client but others as well. It builds on the idea that people impact each other in many ways and that others can be mobilized in efforts of mutual aid. A teacher who helps an angry child in class not only helps the child but relieves her or his own stress, as well as the stress of the other students in the class and of the child's parents. By mapping the child's and others' relationship to "anger," the nature and importance of context is exposed. Everyone involved can join together against "anger," not against the child. Anger becomes the target, not the child.

Narrative helps people understand that the landscape of each of their lives contains many stories, and that the one they are working on, the one that brought them to the social group, or for help, is just one story among many. Narrative sees the person's "landscape of life" as multistoried, containing countless themes, some looming large, like school, a family member's death, a wedding, a success, a failure, an oppressive attack. The subplots of the past often contain the seeds of preferred stories and positive change. Life stories can be changed. Narrative can help gang members to see that there are other subplots in their lives that, if expanded upon, not only shed light on the current story but can help to reauthor or develop new directions: the graffitist who could be an artist, the good student in the group for protection and who may fear doing well in school. A gang, too, is multistoried and should not be seen as a problem but rather as youth brought together as a result of social forces and behaving in ways that can change as the social forces change.

When interviewing is perceived as a conversation with a purpose, members often discover their strengths by, for example, seeing that their commitment to the group helped them or by helping an individual member avoid trouble. This positive action is amplified as a "unique experience." If they could do it once, then a discussion focusing on their ability to modify their behavior toward a desired directions helps them become an audience to their own abilities. "Was there a time when you overcame the call of Al (alcohol) to have a drink with him? Were there times when you might have accepted a challenge by another gang but didn't? Was there a time you became angry in class but didn't hit another child? What were the circumstances? You were able to control your behavior, you can do it, and I and the members will help you."

Another important part of the helping process is writing letters to the individual or group following the meeting. "Your discussion about being harassed by the police, which we talked about at our last meeting, made me think about how difficult it must be to worry about just standing around on the corner talking. Certainly we did it when I was your age. How do you manage not to get abusive to the police when they come along? I wonder if I could keep from being angry? How did that self-control develop? Could we talk about it in the group at our next meeting? I think they would be helped by hearing how you do it." Or in a letter to a teacher, "I have been meeting with Charles for about two weeks, and he is working on ways to keep anger from getting control over him in class. If you see signs of anger starting to get to him, could you just ask him if anger is getting in the way of his participating in class? I think this could be very helpful to him. If I can be of any further assistance, please let me know." The group, too, can write a letter to a member who has been able to take control over his or her life or managed some unique situation. A number of examples of how letters are used in place of records of sessions appears in White and Epston's book, *Narrative Means to Therapeutic Ends*.

## MUTUAL AID

The 1999 AASWG group work standards stated that "Central to social work practice with groups is the concept of mutual aid" (pp. 2-3). But the mutual aid must go beyond the group to include external forces as well. This is supported by research (Kolodny, 1984, pp. 3-5):

after the nature of the relationship between worker and client, external forces are most important in the client's feeling that the help has been successful. What "out there" can help? Support groups, a job, connections with others who are egosyntonic are important sources of mutual aid. If the group members meet outside regular meetings, so much the better. The early pioneering efforts of Ralph Kolodny in Boston to form groups for homebound children was an important precursor of the support group, and a mutual aid success.

In narrative practice, the person's narrative (story) is at the center of practice, not the worker's story (theory). The person's believed story underlies his or her behavior, and we must pay more attention to these stories rather than searching for a form of practice that suggests the problem is within the psyche of the individual. Rather, the problem is externalized. The worker helps the group members formulate the stories they prefer, and members become co-authors in the endeavor; the group itself is faced with making a choice about the story that it would like to be remembered for. These are the bare bones of narrative practice, and they hardly do justice to the differential client-focused action which has evolved from the theories and practice of Foucault, Fanon, and Epston and White. These authors have given us both a philosophy and a practice which is as valuable in work with groups and communities as it is in work with individuals. It is not a therapy in the sense of treatment but a therapy in the sense of social change. White, particularly, has evolved these justice-oriented theories into a practice which alerts practitioners to the power they have to shape the helping scene by minimizing their own storied history and focus on the clients' "landscape" (1988).

The strengths of narrative therapy have led to its full acceptance by the marriage and family counselors and to its preliminary adaptation for use in social work practice. (Hartman, 1995; Laird, 1995; Abels and Abels, 1998). It has shown its strength in the realm of family therapy, where it has become the foremost current approach, and White among others has made use of it as a social action tool on behalf of Australian aborigines and others in total institutions (institutions in which a person's actions are limited by all types of strict rules). His use of narrative as a tool for mutual aid is what makes it most salient for our profession.

Although we have focused on the mutual aid of the members to help each other, it is important to extend the use of mutual aid on be-

rhyming, termination. Phase theory provides a structure but at a price. It can lead the worker to think that all members react similarly. It ignores individualization and diversity. People do not all move at the same pace and rarely at a pace determined by the worker and based on his or her theory (story), or the agency's mandate, or the insurance company's insurance session limit.

## CONCLUSION

Narrative practice does not privilege phases nor time tables. Rather, it looks at a series of reference points: the initial conversation, the naming of the problem, the mapping of the problem's impact on the member and others, the examination of the landscape of the person's life, the making of room for reauthoring, the unique experiences, the reauthoring process which includes support groups, letters, celebrations, the use of the reflecting team when possible. There are numerous checks with the group members on the relevance of the material being covered and their likes and dislikes about the changes that are taking place. Through it all, the worker takes a "know nothing" stance—not that he or she knows nothing about group process or group dynamics but that he or she knows nothing about the meaning of the problem to the person, the meaning of the members to each other, the meaning of membership or of the worker to the member, or even the meaning of the experience to the person. Only the person knows. Remember the women's support group and the incident with the worker who went for the breast transplant; the meaning became clear when she experienced it personally. Only the members know, and meaning must be explored constantly, like an ongoing litmus test.

Social group work has an opportunity to test out, modify, and develop this approach, because it is in an experimental stage with a number of disciplines trying it out and adding to a growing literature about its use. Can we rise beyond our privileged approaches? We have moved to new paradigms before, and we have the skills and ability to do so again.

We see the narrative approach as one that is liberating. It strives to liberate the person from being the problem, being saturated by the problem. It is liberating in that it expands the participants' ability to recognize the limitations that have been placed on them by social forces. It liberates them by helping them find ways to rewrite their stories. It is liberating in that it offers a broader view of their historical subplots. It is liberating to the worker because it supports the idea that she or he doesn't have to have the answers to all problems and need not be an expert. It is liberating because it deals with people's entire lived experience in the landscape of the group's life. It recognizes the importance of providing the client with new knowledge, and that in itself is liberating. It liberates the profession from having a practice for work with individuals and a different practice with groups and communities. It liberates by unifying the profession.

We believe there is much to gain and only a minimal risk in trying out narrative practice. If it doesn't seem right, the members will let you know.

## REFERENCES

Abels, P. and Abels, S.L. (1998). Narratives with Groups: Liberating Practice. Paper given at AASGW Conference, Miami, FL.

Association for the Advancement of Social Work with Groups. (1999). *Standards for Social Work Practice with Groups.* Akron, OH.

Bruner, J.S. (1991). The Narrative Construction of Reality. *Critical Inquiry 18*(1): 1-21.

Dean, R.G. (1998). A Narrative Approach to Groups. *Clinical Social Work Journal 26*(1):1-14.

Fanon, F. (1986). *The Wretched of the Earth.* New York: Grove Press.

Foucault, M. (1980). *Power/Knowledge: Selected Interviews and Other Writings, 1972-1977.* Gordon (Ed. and trans.). New York: Pantheon.

Gleick, J. (1999). *Faster.* New York: Pantheon Press.

Hartman, A. (1995). Ideological Themes in Family Policy. *Families in Society 76* (3):182-192.

Illich, I. (1973). *Tools for Conviviality.* New York: Harper and Row Publishers.

Kolodny, R. (1984). Guest Editorial. *Social Work with Groups 7*(4):3-5.

Laird, J. (1995). Family-Centered Practice in the Postmodern Era. *Families in Society 76*(3):150-162.

Maram, M. (1998). Breast Cancer: A Personal and Professional Crisis. *Reflections: Narratives of Professional Helping 5*(1):39-45.

The Power of Our Journeys. (1996). *Adelaide Family Therapy Newsletter,* Summer, pp. 1-16.

Quines, E. (1991). Managers Tell Stories. *The New York Times,* August 1, Section 3, p. 4.

Rushdie, S. (1995). Lecture: A Thousand Days in a Balloon. Long Beach, CA.

Schwartz, W. (1961). The Social Worker with the Group. *The Social Welfare Forum, 1961* (pp. 146-177). New York: Columbia University Press.

Tuckman, B.W. (1965). Developmental Sequence in Small Groups. *Psychological Bulletin, LXIII*, pp. 384-399.

Wakefield, J.C. (1966). Does Social Work Need the Eco-Systems Perspective? *Social Service Review 70*(2):1-31.

Weiner, J. (1999). *Time, Love, Memory.* New York: Vintage Books.

White, M. (1989). The Externalization of the Problem and the Re-Authoring of Lives and Relationships. *Dulwich Center Newsletter,* Summer, pp. 3-20.

White, M. (1994). Quoted by O'Hanlon, B. *The Third Wave: The Family Therapy Networker 18*(6):18-26.

White, M. (1995). *Re-Authoring Lives: Interviews and Essays.* Adelaide, Australia: Dulwich Centre Publications.

White, M. and Epston, D. (1990). *Narrative Means to Therapeutic Ends.* New York: W.W. Norton.

Chapter 5

# Citizens, Victims, and Offenders Restoring Justice: A Prison-Based Group Work Program Bridging the Divide

Madeline L. Lovell
Jacqueline B. Helfgott
Charles Lawrence

In recent years, the criminal justice system has shifted away from rehabilitation of offenders toward a more punitive approach. Researchers note that the involvement of professional social workers in such settings as community corrections declined in tandem with this rising focus on punishment (Goodman, 1997), beginning in the 1980s. Social work's emphasis on actualizing human potential and respecting the worth and dignity of all people at times appears at odds with the retributive climate of today's criminal justice environment. Given the extent to which oppressed groups are represented in the inmate population, the lack of social work influence in criminal justice is to be regretted.

However, emerging models for achieving justice offer opportunities for social work to contribute to this field in a manner congruent with professional social work values and ethics. Falling under the rubric of "restorative justice" programs, these interventions define crime as a serious form of interpersonal conflict (McCold, 1996; Zehr, 1990) affecting the victim, offender, and the local community. The focus is less on the violation of law than on the damage done to interpersonal relationships and the property of those harmed. This

The research reported in this chapter was funded by the Center on Crime, Communities, and Culture of the Open Society Institute, New York.

chapter describes a prison-based restorative justice program entitled Citizens, Victims, and Offenders Restoring Justice (CVORJ) designed to provide non-related offenders and victims with opportunities to restore victim-offender relationships, to educate offenders about the experience of victims, and to facilitate the healing process. The program also attempted to change community attitudes by inviting interested citizens to participate, thus offering them new ways of thinking about crime and justice. Social group work theory will be applied to inform understanding of group development and to suggest appropriate intervention strategies.

Citizens, Victims, and Offenders Restoring Justice was a pilot program conducted at the Washington State Reformatory in 1997-1998. Its purpose was to develop, implement, and evaluate a seminar on restorative justice involving victims, offenders, and citizens. The seminar addressed issues of offender accountability, victim's rights, and community participation in the justice process in a way that balanced victim and offender rights and interests with attention to citizen involvement and concern. Three separate seminars, each ten to twelve weeks in duration, were conducted over the time of this pilot study.

## SELECTION AND INDUCTION OF PARTICIPANTS

A target group consisting of eight victims, eight offenders, and eight community members was sought for each seminar. Flyers were distributed to inmates in the general population at the Washington State Reformatory. Thirty (ten per seminar) of the fifty inmates who applied were selected after completing questionnaires and interviews. Criteria for inclusion were nature of criminal and infraction history, ability to work well in a group, willingness to discuss past offenses, and understanding of and openness to victims' concerns. Flyers soliciting victim and community participants were distributed to victims' advocacy organizations, local community colleges, and universities. Interested people were interviewed by telephone. Volunteers reported that family and friends felt participation would be upsetting, not understanding that many victims experience an ongoing need to be listened to in order to heal.

Twenty-seven male offenders ranging in age from twenty-two to fifty-seven (X = 39) years participated in the project. Seventeen were white, eight African American, and two Hispanic. Most were incarcerated for violent crimes. Twenty of the offenders (74 percent) were serving time for murder; three of these were also convicted of rape. Three of the offenders were convicted of attempted murder, two for multiple robberies, one for burglary, and one for drug offenses. Their mean sentence was 40.8 years and ranged from 5 years to Life Without Parole. The eighteen victim participants (fifteen female and three male) ranged in age from twenty-two to seventy-eight (X = 41.3) years. Fourteen were white, two African American, one Asian American, and one Native American. Five were family members of homicide victims. One was a family member of a kidnap/rape victim. Six were victims of rape or sexual assault, three of burglary, one of aggravated assault, and two of domestic violence/assault. On average, twelve years had elapsed since their victimization. Finally, fifteen community members (ten female and five male) participated. They ranged in age from twenty-one to sixty-two (X = 28.9) years. Thirteen were white, one Hispanic, and one East Indian.

There were relatively few dropouts. A male victim and a female community member (a couple) withdrew after the first session of Seminar 1. A second victim, offended by comments made by community members, withdrew from the program after the sixth session of Seminar 3. Two offenders were transferred to other institutions. Another inmate withdrew after the first session of Seminar 1 to avoid being strip-searched following sessions. The final inmate to quit cited personal reasons.

Separate preseminar orientations for inmates and outside participants were conducted one week prior to the first session of each seminar to introduce the program and allow the opportunity to ask questions. "Outsiders" were informed of corrections policy and completed necessary paperwork.

## INTERVENTION MODEL

The preliminary phases of group work have been found to be critical to the creation of a viable program (Shulman, 1999; Zastrow, 1989; Anderson, 1997; Northern, 1970). This was particularly true in this instance. Prison management is a highly politicized and contentious issue in Washington state. Victims' groups are politically powerful. Because one of the hopes for the project was to forge linkages between polarized groups, a strategy was needed to begin to build a sense of community and engender support for the project in and outside the prison. To that end, a committee comprised of fifteen representatives from various organizations (Helfgott, Lovell, and Lawrence, in press) was invited to consult on the development of the seminar format. Victim advocacy groups, victim-offender mediation agencies, university researchers, high-ranking prison administrators, and offenders were represented. The three offenders selected were Lifers who had achieved respect and high-status positions within the institution.

The central organizing feature of the seminars themselves was the sharing of personal crime experiences by all members. The use of personal narrative as a powerful tool for interpersonal and community change has been a key aspect of models designed to bring down walls between opposing groups. Such interventions include community building, community peacemaking, and cross-racial/international dialogues (Peck, 1987; Fisher, 1997; Saunders, 1999; Rothman, 1997). Narratives inform our understanding of the "webs of meaning" or context within which humans act (Personal Narratives Group, 1989, p. 19). The sharing of recollections of significant life history allows for the reframing of difficult situations and the possibility of new interpretations (White and Epston, 1990; Baldwin, 1998). It empowers individuals by reducing isolation and enhancing the recognition of possible avenues for change (Hopps and Pinderhughes, 1999), providing "validation through collective experience" (Gutierrez, Parsons, and Cox, 1998, p. 4). Group members see that others have confronted similar challenges and learn from each other's coping strategies. Storytelling also has been used very effectively with students of a variety of ages to aid in the development of moral imagination (Coles, 1989). Within the criminal justice arena, victim offender mediation programs have found the recounting of personal crime narratives to be a potent tool to enhance understanding, to bring about attitude change, and to facilitate healing (Van Ness and Strong, 1997).

A final critical aspect of the intervention was the provision of support, particularly for victims. Each week an outside committee member attended to monitor the safety and well-being of outside participants and provided whatever support was required. Participants also sought help from the facilitator between sessions, sharing thoughts, reflections, even dreams. Offender committee members were available to support inmates between sessions and to broker their concerns.

## SESSION CONTENT

Three different seminar trials were held at the Washington State Reformatory between September 1997 and July 1998. The format constructed by the committee was implemented in Seminar 1. Minor changes were made to Seminars 2 and 3 as a result of group feedback. Sessions were held in the Visitors' Annex, as prison staff decided that entering the actual prison might be too upsetting for victims. The principal investigator of the study served as lead facilitator. The researcher collecting participant observation data attended each week and acted as cofacilitator. Each seminar was followed by a focus group and by a voluntary tour of the prison.

The first two sessions of Seminar 1 focused on building connections between members and introducing the principles of restorative justice. Members were asked to write on a 3 × 5 card their greatest hopes and fears for the seminar. The cards were shuffled and passed out for another person to read aloud. The anonymity of this exercise deepened personal sharing in the face of significant personal anxiety. When asked how they felt about being present, participants talked of how difficult it was and how frightened they were. A check-in was held at the beginning of all sessions to allow sharing of reactions.

Information on restorative justice was drawn from readings in the text, *Restoring Justice.* Central themes included responsibility, accountability, reparation, restoration, reconstruction, and reintegration. The sharing of personal narratives began in the third week. Participants were asked to share their own experience of crime focusing on the circumstances leading up to the crime, the crime itself, and the harms caused. Each week one victim, one offender, and one community member shared their personal crime narrative, reflecting on what they would consider justice.

Participants were then encouraged to relate the central themes of restorative justice to each crime story. They were asked to consider such questions as: What needs to be done to restore the harm done? Is it possible to restore the harms resulting from violent crimes or from homicide (Getzel and Masters, 1983)? Whose responsibility is it to make things right? What does justice mean? What does it mean for offenders to be responsible/accountable for their crimes? What might an offender do while in prison to help repair the damage caused by his/her crime? What commonalities exist among participants? What stigmas do victims and offenders experience in the aftermath of crime? What does the public want from offenders? Do community members "owe" victims and offenders anything? What does it mean for community members to be responsible/accountable with respect to the needs of victims and offenders? What could be done to make justice more meaningful?

The most challenging aspect of the format for both participants and facilitators was having sufficient time to allow participants to respond in depth to each crime narrative. In order to meet this difficulty, the theoretical discussion of restorative justice was shortened to one session in Seminar 2. Storytelling began in the second session. Reading materials were distributed at orientation to give participants an extra week to begin reading, and a syllabus was prepared. Additional readings on exoffender reintegration (Helfgott, 1997), forgiveness (Ross, 1998), and public perceptions (Gorczyk and Perry, 1997) were distributed midseminar. Seminar 3 maintained this general outline but was extended to twelve weeks.

## *GROUP PROCESS THEMES*

As noted above, the same general outline and preorientation procedures were followed in each seminar. However, because storytelling formed the basis for the majority of discussions, each seminar was greatly influenced by member composition. Thus, the developmental process of each seminar differed. Also, each stressed slightly different areas of the common content. Seminar 1 was marked by the greatest leader anxiety as well as the resolution of conflict leading to a marked sense of group cohesion. Seminar 2 participants demonstrated more comfort from the initial stages. Members showed a high level of energy and enthusiasm for attempting systemic change. Gender issues became an evident subtheme. Seminar 3 was characterized by unresolved conflict that contributed to a sense of "stuckness" and despair. The following brief description of the elements of group process will highlight the differences between seminars.

In Seminar 1, the effect of bringing together the three constituencies in an open forum was unknown. Anxiety and ambivalence were predominant in the first session of the first seminar, as would be expected in the beginning phase of a group (Shulman, 1999; Henry, 1992; Zastrow, 1989). As victims and community members waited to pass through the scanner into the visiting area before the first session, they seemed very subdued. When asked in the session how they felt coming to this first meeting, all shared significant discomfort. Inmates worried that one group would be outnumbered, visitors would be stressed by prison security, they as offenders would not be accepted, no one would show up, and/or they might be strip-searched. Victim and community members shared uneasiness about walking through the visitors' room and concern that the "topics are not safe topics." One victim stated that "It was hard, very hard to come . . . very scary."

Conflict then gradually emerged. First, tension developed between the three inmate committee members and the facilitator. Accustomed to exerting influence in the prison, these Lifers dominated discussions, not hearing victim concerns. One offender committee member, a very physically imposing man, repeatedly interrupted others despite clear ground rules. By session 4, the three men overtly challenged the authority of the lead facilitator in private conversation, suggesting that the leadership of the group should rotate to them. Facilitators asserted that this would not happen and emphasized that interruptions would not be tolerated. The reaffirmation of structured rules and leader control appeared to be reassuring. Inmates, accustomed to the authoritarian structure of the prison, ceased challenging the facilitator. Victims and community members relaxed.

Second, early in the seminar a victim challenged an offender's statement about the pointlessness of the death penalty by replying under her breath, ". . . Executing the offender gives healing to the victims, it is healing and should be done within two years. . . ." Inmates responded by cutting her off, saying loudly that her point of view was vengeance. The cofacilitator refocused the group on the ground rules, noting that everyone had agreed upon the critical role of honest sharing for this program to work. Subsequent discussion was characterized by respect on both sides and careful listening. Inmates were pleased that this participant over time showed them greater warmth, although her opinion on this issue remained unchanged.

Third, several very quiet student community members frustrated others by their failure to contribute. These young students found the stories of crime and suffering overwhelming. A turning point occurred in Session 4 when members shared their uncertainty regarding their role and their fear of being intrusive because the stories seemed "none of their business." This spotlighted the role of community both in the group and in society in responding to crime. Community members were acknowledged as vital and encouraged to share the personal impact of what they were hearing.

As these arenas of disagreement and conflict were clarified, anxiety subsided. The working through of anxiety and conflict fostered a greater equilibrium (Henry, 1992) marked by a sense of increasing intimacy and cohesion (Northen, 1970). As people recounted their experiences, a bond formed among members. A dominant theme in this group was the exploration of commonalities across labels. Most felt that they had experienced the roles of both victimized and victimizer. Participants' interactions also reflected deepening cohesion. On at least two occasions, inmates rose to fetch Kleenex for victims who were tearful. Subsequently, a victim who had seemed quite hostile to offenders offered a Kleenex to a distraught offender after much thought. Finally, several inmates came up to the same man, hugging him in a very marked gesture of support.

After a two-week Christmas break, this sense of "we-ness" appeared to be set back. In this seventh session, one inmate recounted a confusing, vague crime history, seemingly denying responsibility. Only another offender challenged him, although all the members had very similar and negative reactions to his story. The group was reluctant to disturb the bond by risking confrontation. It wasn't until the final session that the group joined in challenging an inmate's story— possibly a doorknob effect (Shulman, 1999). Given that the tasks of the seminar included holding inmates accountable, participants appeared blocked from fully engaging in the work of the group.

In Seminar 2, a wider range of age and experience fostered a more relaxed and lively group process from the beginning. This greater ease had two likely sources. First, the facilitators were less anxious. Second, many of the participants were acquainted with each other. Student participants were both enthusiastic and open; older participants were striking in their lack of bitterness. Members challenged inmates more to take responsibility for their crimes. Discussion centered on the healing process and how offenders could demonstrate remorse. The work of the group in Seminar 2 was facilitated by the manner in which the first stories were shared. As the first inmate to speak disclosed details of the murder he had committed, he modeled a norm of honesty and believability. Because of his openness and approachability, outsiders were able to raise questions even in response to this first story. The victim who shared that first evening was also extremely articulate, reinforcing the beginning made by the offender.

Although the leadership struggles evident in the first seminar did not reemerge, tensions still existed. Underlying concerns included questions about offender responsibility and honesty as well as issues of personal safety. Only in subgroups, when victims and community members met together in the post-session debriefing or when inmates talked among themselves between sessions, did the full range of reactions get expressed. It remained easier to make supportive comments than to challenge each other in the large group. Nonetheless, while it was frightening, participants in the second seminar did take steps earlier to create a group climate that valued challenging questions. Interestingly, inmates were the first to do so. By the fourth session, inmates confronted each other on narrative accuracy and sincerity, providing helpful modeling for the other participants.

Participants were able to support each other in surprising ways. For example, when one offender who was very frightened about revealing the nature of his crime did talk, other offenders approached him at the break, putting their arms around him. Inmates were also able to give powerful messages to victims, for instance, "You had no responsibility—it was all on him. Rape is not a sex crime. It is a crime of violence, power, dominance. . . . You were alive in the wrong place at the wrong time."

Seminar 3 was the most difficult to lead because participants failed to resolve the conflict/disequilibrium stage to achieve a sense of themselves as a unified group. Victims, offenders, and community members instead seemed mired in tensions that simmered under the surface. A basic sense of safety seemed to be lacking. In this group, not only were some inmates more emotionally defended, but many of the outsiders were justice professionals (two parole officers, a police officer, five victim advocates). Interactions appeared to be determined by participants' social and vocational roles and were characterized by less empathy. Three victim advocates appeared particularly hesitant about the seminar's usefulness. Sitting together and interacting primarily with each other, they were perceived by others as a clique. One of these women complained in secret early in the seminar to the head of the state Department of Corrections that the project was too offender oriented. Prison officials relayed this information but required that nothing be said. Yet her desire to shape the experience toward her own agenda significantly influenced group dynamics. Facilitators and participants held unstated frustrations that impaired their ability to act effectively. Achieving an open sharing of concerns in order to clarify purpose would likely have reduced tension (Henry, 1992).

In a similar vein, a victim who had suffered an assault only weeks before the seminar presented as emotionally very fragile. She became upset when an inmate failed to understand the experience of being victimized. Stating that he was victim blaming, she began to cry and left the session accompanied by an advocate. She attended sporadically after this incident but declined to withdraw despite encouragement to do so. When she was present, people appeared to be even more cautious in expressing themselves, fearing to distress her. Yet many participants were privately very critical of her story, believing that she had put herself at needless risk. This situation contributed to an unstated norm of unconditional acceptance of the veracity and completeness of victims' stories. Questioning how they might have endangered themselves was taboo. Facilitators were unclear how best to respond, not wishing to revictimize yet aware of negative group dynamics.

In general, participants in the final seminar were less hopeful and more worried about causing offense. The difficulty in moving to a more advanced stage of group development seemed in large part a function of the mix of participants. Bringing together criminal justice professionals, victim advocates, and violent offenders (at least two of whom appeared to view themselves more as victims) made an uneasy blend. Even extending the number of sessions from ten to twelve was insufficient to bridge the divide. The strain erupted in the final sessions when an offender refused to discuss the crime for which he was incarcerated. Members felt manipulated when he subsequently gave two women the name of a book describing the crime—a particularly heinous murder—showing little awareness of the impact of his action on the group. Victims and community members demanded that he be removed from the group. Inmates were more tolerant, seeing him as simply not ready for a deeper level of honesty. In retrospect, it is clear that this man was the target of group scapegoating. It was safer for the group to condemn his hidden agenda than to challenge victim participants who had also not been fully honest.

## CHALLENGES TO THE DEVELOPMENT
## OF GROUP COHESION

As noted above, the seminars in many respects followed classical stages of group development. This was particularly true of the first two seminars. From the preorientation activities, participants followed a path of initial anxiety about what would happen through a stage of conflict to reach a more cohesive point where bonding among members and a dedication to the tasks of the group became hallmarks of the experience. However, this model offered unique challenges to the achievement of a sense of connection between people. These included the large number of participants per seminar, personal safety versus honesty, gender issues, and confidentiality concerns.

First, the large number of participants in each seminar made the development of bonds difficult. There was not enough time for all members to share their thoughts and feelings. Quiet members could and did remain so throughout, becoming little known to the others. Utilizing smaller subgroups for discussion would have offered a solution. However, participants did not want to divide up because everyone wanted to hear all the conversation. Ironically, the more comfortable people became, the more they wanted to talk. Another possibility would have been to limit the group size. Yet, given how polarized the constituencies were, having fewer than six or eight members from each seemed too small. Fluctuations in attendance might negatively unbalance sessions.

Second, the very nature of the program limited the extent to which intimate sharing was both possible and/or desirable. Sharing was limited solely to crime experiences. The inmates had been incarcerated for very serious crimes, and there was no guarantee that they had changed. Offenders quickly learn in prison the vocabulary of repentance. Very real rewards are linked to the extent to which they can convince others of their sincerity. Adequate protections must be available to protect outside participants from revictimization or manipulation. Participants were told not to share last names or addresses. Ongoing contact between inmates and outsiders was not permitted. The maintenance of boundaries between inmates and the rest of the group proved to be one of the most important facilitator tasks. Many victims and community members were quickly struck by the men's apparent normality and sincerity. The development of a false sense of security— losing sight of risks inherent in these contacts— posed dangers. Yet achievement of program goals required people to move beyond stereotypes and see each other's common humanity.

Third, gender issues complicated group dynamics in several ways. The offenders were all male. Most of the outside participants were female. Facilitators speculated that the difficulty victims and community members had in being confrontive might be gender linked. Also, correctional settings function as hierarchical, semimilitary organizations. Inmates were unaccustomed to and likely confused by a feminist style of leadership that invites collaboration. Finally, many men in a correctional setting develop relationships with female volunteers and staff. Although not encouraged, it is in fact common practice. In this program, offenders were warned not to attempt to establish relationships with women participants. Even so, four men offered notes surreptitiously to one of the victims on a prison tour. She immediately told the facilitator, and the men were reprimanded.

Finally, confidentiality was a concern because it was associated with personal safety for inmates. Inmates frequently do not talk of their crimes after incarceration. In a number of instances, the details of an offender's crime were unknown to the general prison population. The men were frightened that widespread knowledge of certain types of crime, namely those against women and children and any sex crimes, would affect their status as well as their safety in "the yard."

## RECOMMENDATIONS AND CONCLUSIONS

In conclusion, programs of this nature offer social work practitioners an opportunity to apply group work theory and skills in promising new fields of service. Focused on repairing the harms caused by crime and the reintegration into society of both victims and offenders, restorative justice programs not only offer opportunities to help victims and offenders heal but also provide new opportunities for community development. Interested community members gain an opportunity to consider how to become active in addressing issues related to violence and crime today.

Recommendations for future programs would include careful recruitment and screening of participants, clear consequences for violations of ground rules, and consideration of ways to model normative behaviors in the group. Continued screening of inmates for primitive defense mechanisms, inability to experience empathy, and unwillingness to admit guilt is essential. Ideally, *The Psychopathy Checklist* (Hare, 1991) would be the preferred screening tool. Outside participants should be screened for their willingness to share their own humanity. Community members with greater life experience should be recruited for the wisdom they can bring to the program. Based on this experience, a postvictimization waiting period to guide the selection of victim-participants would be beneficial. Finally, participants from diverse racial and ethnic backgrounds should be sought to increase cultural sensitivity. One frustration experienced by program staff was the extent to which the focus on personal responsibility failed to account for issues of oppression and disadvantage. Broadening the seminar's attention to incorporate a societal injustice dimension could enhance the relevance of the discussion for people from oppressed groups.

## REFERENCES

Anderson, J. (1997). *Social work with groups: A process model.* New York: Longman.

Baldwin, C. (1998). *Calling the circle.* New York: Bantam.

Coles, R. (1989). *The call of stories.* Boston, MA: Houghton Mifflin.

Fisher, R.J. (1997). *Interactive conflict resolution.* Syracuse, NY: Syracuse University Press.

Getzel, G.S. and Masters, R. (1983). Group work with parents of homicide victims. *Social Work with Groups* 6(2):81-92.

Goodman, H. (1997). Social group work in community corrections. *Social Work with Groups* 20(1):51-64.

Gorczyk, J.F. and Perry, J.G. (1997). What the public wants: Market research finds support for restorative justice. *Corrections Today* 59(December):78-83.

Gutierrez, L.M., Parsons, R.J., and Cox, E.O. (1998). *Empowerment in social work practice.* Pacific Grove, CA: Brooks/Cole.

Hare, R.D. (1991). *The psychopathy checklist* (Revised edition). North Tonawanda, NY: Multi-Health Systems.

Helfgott, J. (1997). Ex-offender needs versus community opportunity in Seattle, Washington. *Federal Probation* 61(2):12-24.

Helfgott, J., Lovell, M., and Lawrence, C. (in press). The development of the Citizens, Victims, and Offenders Restoring Justice program at the Washington State Reformatory. *Criminal Justice Policy Review.*

Henry, S. (1992). *Group skills in social work* (Second edition). Pacific Grove, CA: Brooks/Cole.

Hopps, J.G. and Pinderhughes, E. (1999). *Group work with overwhelmed clients.* New York: The Free Press.

McCold, P. (1996). Restorative justice and the role of community. In B. Galaway and J. Hudson (Eds.), *Restorative justice: International perspectives* (pp. 85-102). Monsey, NY: Criminal Justice Press.

Northen, H. (1970). *Social work with groups.* New York: Columbia University Press.

Peck, M.S. (1987). *The different drum.* New York: Simon and Schuster.

Personal Narratives Group (Eds.) (1989). *Interpreting women's lives.* Bloomington, IN: University of Indiana Press.

Ross, M.B. (1998). Forgiveness: What it is not. *The Mennonite,* February 24, pp. 8-10.

Rothman, J. (1997). *Resolving identity-based conflict.* San Francisco: Jossey-Bass.

Saunders, H.H. (1999). *A public peace process.* New York: St. Martin's Press.

Shulman, L. (1999). *Skills of helping individuals, families, and small groups.* Itasca, IL: F.E. Peacock.

Van Ness, D. and Strong, K.H. (1997). *Restoring justice.* Cincinnati, OH: Anderson Publishing.

White, M. and Epston, D. (1990). *Narrative means to therapeutic ends.* New York: W.W. Norton.

Zastrow, C. (1989). *Social work with groups* (Second edition). Chicago, IL: Nelson-Hall.

Zehr, H. (1990). *Changing lenses.* Scottsdale, AZ: Herald Press.

Chapter 6

# Gender Diversity: A Powerful Tool for Enriching Group Experience

Robin Edward Gearing

A basic groupwork axiom dictates that the formidable therapeutic value of the group experience and process emerges from the richness of the group itself. The individually unique resources of each group, when effectively drawn upon and explored, can augment the recognized therapeutic factors, thereby increasing the potential for each group member and the group as a whole. A fundamental and often underutilized resource within groupwork, and one of the basic elements of group composition, is gender diversity.

This chapter is organized around the following objectives: to identify significant differences in male/female affect and behavior in small groups; to examine the impact of these differences on small group processes; and, finally, to demonstrate how the group facilitator may apply this knowledge of gender diversity to enhance both the individual experience within the group and the group process as a whole.

These objectives will be accomplished by assessing different components of gender-related issues, responses, and diversity. Also, there will be an examination of the nature of gender diversity through the development of a matrix that compares and contrasts female and male differences along a number of determinants, variables, and domains. Several strategies for intervention and implications for practice will be accentuated for effective application within groupwork.

## DIVERSITY IN GROUP

Through its unique history and development, groupwork has been consistently demonstrated to be an effective method of addressing individual concerns, issues, and needs (Rutan and Stone, 1993; Corey and Corey, 1992; Ormont, 1992; Yalom, 1985). Furthermore, the nature, process, and composition of the therapeutic group creates a dynamic environment that can encourage individual growth, development, and change (Yalom, 1998; Shulman, 1992; Brown, 1991; Rose, 1989). Today, group treatment is recognized as a valuable therapeutic tool to address diversity, as it has the advantage of being a microcosm that reflects the larger cultural and societal diversities (Shaw and Barrett-Power, 1998; Brown and Mistry, 1994; Feld and Urman-Klein, 1993; Husle, 1985).

In every group, regardless of its similarities or homogenous nature, diversity and differences will exist. It is often out of this diversity, which is created when several individuals join together in a group, that much of the therapeutic value of this modality emerges. One of the most fundamental diversities that has received little attention in groupwork is gender (Goldberger, 1996; Garvin and Reed, 1983; Martin and Shanahan, 1983). Gender diversity can be a powerful tool for enriching the group experience. This element can be readily ignored or minimized in the name of equity, or negatively fostered to promote oppression, stagnation, and inequalities. Although worthy of focus, the central nature of this chapter does not review gender diversity as a means to promote equality or level the playing field. Rather, it seeks to positively recognize many of the differences inherent in gender diversity and to therapeutically utilize their implications for expanding and enriching the group experience.

## Gendered Patterns in Group

The effect of gender diversity on groupwork will be elaborated through the exploration of nine areas where significant differences between male and female experiences have been noted both in the literature and in this author's professional experience. These nine dimensions reflect a difference in either a behavioral or an affective response that may be useful as a resource for attaining individual or group goals. These "clinically observable patterns" regarding different gender responses are offered without value or judgment on their respective natures. Furthermore, they do not reflect the individual variations that will occur within these patterns. This chapter does not attempt to identify a "better" response but recognizes differences

(Garvin and Reed, 1983) and how their potential can be positively incorporated without moral interpretation or judgment into the group processes.

## *Impact of Gender Patterns in Groupwork*

If something is part of group therapy, then it affects the process. Whether that something is an issue, an emotion, or a topic raised, the physical environment, the number of participants, the nature of the group modality, the theory applied, or the comfort level of the group facilitator, the processes within the group are affected. The specific effect is determined by the uniqueness and the number of variables in the group and can be dramatic or minimal, positive or negative. Gender patterns affect a group. In discussing the concept of process in group, Irvin Yalom stated the following: "The group therapist endeavors to understand what a particular sequence reveals about the relationship between one patient and the other group members, or between clusters or cliques of members, or between the members and the leader, or, finally, between the group as a whole and its primary task" (1998, p. 46).

The clinically observable gender patterns, like group dynamics, are not fixed or rigid. They are subject to differences of group and in group. Also, they are inevitably affected by a variety of factors including the individuality of every group member; nonetheless, they impact upon the group process and each participant. Therefore, it is important that a group therapist recognizes, monitors, and is aware of not only the gendered patterns and their impacts on group processes but also their potential for clinical implications.

## *DIFFERENTIAL RESPONSES AND THEIR IMPLICATIONS FOR PRACTICE*

The nine dimensions include: task versus process orientation, conflict/competition, collaboration/cooperation, relational style/connection to others, communication style, power/assertiveness, self-disclosure, anger, and shame. These dimensions, outlined in Table 6.1, will compare and contrast the male/female response in small groupwork.

TABLE 6.1. Male/Female Responses Across Nine Dimensions

| Dimension | Male Response | Female Response |
|---|---|---|
| 1. Task versus Process Orientation | • Traditionally more task or action oriented.<br>• More readily able to engage and relate through tasks. | • Traditionally more process oriented.<br>• Can engage and relate openly within processes. |
| 2. Conflict/ Competition | • Used more often and with greater ease by men.<br>• A means to grow and connect with others and the group. | • Minimized and difficult for women.<br>• Often leads to disconnection and disenfranchisement. |
| 3. Collaboration/ Cooperation | • Inhibits men's engagement in the group processes.<br>• Can be seen as threatening to their individuality. | • Enables engagement and connection to others and investment in the group processes. |
| 4. Relational Style/ Connections | • Viewed as hierarchical with an emphasis on privacy.<br>• Feelings of inadequacy may lead to withdrawal or attack. | • Often look for and want to connect with others.<br>• Explore relationships as a way to value and express self. |
| 5. Communication Style | • More difficult to directly express feelings or affect.<br>• Less skilled at empathic listening and nonverbal cues. | • Able to connect and affirm with others through communication.<br>• Use to negotiate agreement and to lessen disagreement. |
| 6. Power/ Assertiveness | • Socialization may facilitate and ease male use of power.<br>• Men more able to be direct in being assertive/powerful. | • Group may reflect larger disparity of power between genders and quiet women.<br>• Seen as "less" feminine. |
| 7. Self-Disclosure | • Taught through socialization that expressing feelings can be seen as weak or feminine.<br>• Difficulty expressing affect. | • More able to share and connect through emotions.<br>• Expectations for growth, relief, and comfort via self-disclosure. |
| 8. Anger | • Anger is an acceptable emotion for men to safely express.<br>• Expression of anger often taps into other emotions for men. | • Women's expression of anger has been silenced through culture and socialization.<br>• The use of anger in interpersonal interaction is less acceptable for women. |
| 9. Shame | • Men tend to withdraw from humiliation or attack with aggression when experiencing shame. | • Women often use depression to cope with anger.<br>• More able to cope with shame through sharing of affect. |

These responses will highlight recognized differences from the male and female perspective. However, it is important to note that these responses are only generally recognizable patterns, and they do not imply gender typology, stereotypes, or absolutes.

### *Dimension One: Task versus Process Orientation*

A frequently observed gender dimension in groupwork concerns the task versus process orientation of individuals. This internal dimension of behavior is repeatedly broken down in the literature along gender lines, specifically in noting that females tend to be more process oriented, while men favor a task or action orientation (Golden, 1997; Wilbur and Roberts-Wilbur, 1994; Feld and Urman-Klein, 1993). The impact and clarity of this gender difference appears to be decreasing as traditional role definitions and socialization are being both challenged and deconstructed (Pollack, 1995; Carter and McGoldrick, 1988). While the impact of this factor may be lessening, it remains to some extent that men are more able to engage through tasks and females are more comfortable engaging with other group members and the larger group through the process.

The implication for practice regarding task versus process orientation can be used as a valuable tool to enrich both individual experience and the group process as a whole. Group facilitators with awareness of differing gender responses may have better success engaging group members by encouraging men to connect through tasks and women via the processes. Also, awareness of this dimension may facilitate not only the initial formation of the group process but also the working and ending stages of group development.

### *Dimensions Two and Three: Conflict/Competition and Collaboration/Cooperation*

Conflict and competition represent a behavioral dimension that reflects differing female/male responses within groupwork. Wallach (1994, p. 29) noted that "competition is a universal group phenomenon" that is revealed and experienced differently by women and men. It has often been reported that women avoid, take responsibility, and disconnect from others in conflict or competition (Ewashen, 1997; Wallach, 1994; Hertzel, Barton, and Davenport, 1994). It has been further suggested that women defer struggles in group in order to enhance group cohesion and increase individual time in group (Wallach, 1994; Alonso and Rutan, 1979). Conversely, the task-oriented nature and aggressiveness of competition or conflict is more useful for men within the group structure. While competition and conflict may be disconnecting for women, it is often a connective element for men.

The third dimension of gender diversity is that of collaboration and cooperation. The early socialization of males to autonomy and independence over connectiveness and interpersonal dependency tends to inhibit and minimize cooperation and collaboration with others (Lavent, 1996; Pollack, 1995). Men initially distrust and question cooperation until it is seen as nonthreatening to their individuality. The female response to collaboration and cooperation facilitates quicker investment in, connection to, and engagement with other members and the larger group processes (Wallach, 1994; Burden and Gottlieb, 1987; Schubert Walker, 1987).

The identified dimensions of "conflict/competition" and "collaboration/cooperation" offer numerous applications for enriching the group experience. Again, when appropriate in group, the facilitator may bring these dimensions to the awareness of the participants, thereby encouraging discussion on these specific issues, or use these patterns to address, clarify, or process individual affect or behaviors unique to that group. In a group conducted by this author, the members were relating how they were parented, which led to an affect-laden discussion. The dynamics of the group resulted in some of the identified gender-patterned responses regarding conflict and collaboration. When the facilitator directly raised these observable patterns, group members were able to relate them to their own issues and note both patterns and differing processes within the group and between various members. The group members noted this interpersonal interaction as an opportunity, which unexpectedly encouraged growth without concerns regarding the feared potential judgment.

### Dimensions Four and Five: Relational Style/Connections and Communicative Style

Another behavioral dimension observed in group and reflective of gender diversity is the participants' relational style and connection to others. Although seemingly stereotypical, men's relationships and connection to others has been reported as hierarchical, with an emphasis on privacy (Wilbur and Roberts-Wilbur, 1994; Wright, 1994). It has been further observed that these male characteristics can raise feelings of inadequacy that may result in withdrawal or attacking of others (Pollack, 1998; Wright, 1994; Franklin, 1984). Females seem to want and be more able to explore and utilize relationship connections as a means of valuing self, normalizing, and enabling autonomous self-expression (Ewashen, 1997; Wright and Gould, 1996).

A further behavioral trait, and the fifth dimension differentiating male and female behavior in small groups, is communication style. It has been frequently described that men have more difficulty than women in the direct expression of feelings or affect (Wright, 1994; Feld and Urman-Klein, 1993; Tannen, 1990). Furthermore, females are more able to facilitate connections and affirm others through direct, open interpersonal communications (Schubert Walker, 1987; Brody, 1987). Also, women are more able to openly negotiate similarities and agreement, while diminishing disagreements (Khan, 1996; Tannen, 1990). In contrast to women, communication patterns for men seem to lack empathic listening and appreciation of nonverbal cues (Brooks, 1996).

The gender-patterned responses that focus around the dimensions of "relational style/connections" and "communications" present several implications for practice within small groupwork. Also, these dimensions are frequently connected to group topics and the individual concerns or issues that brought members into treatment. A prerequisite for effective group treatment is interpersonal interaction and communication between all participants, members, and facilitators in the group. Therefore, how individuals communicate has a dramatic and direct, as well as indirect, effect on the group process as a whole and on each member.

Facilitators who are aware of differences in gender diversity can enrich and encourage group members to grow by noting aspects of observable patterns as they develop and emerge in group. Examples of patterns can further be used to promote discussion and exploration. Some examples may include the following: (a) is it easier for you as a male/female to be more direct when talking to others? (b) does the characteristic of power tend to be more feminine or masculine in nature? (c) are all interactions or connections with others based on power or some type of hierarchy? (d) if someone is assertive with you, are you more likely as a female/male to become quieter or asser-tive back? (e) can or should differences in gender affect how each of us in group communicates with each other? How a group facilitator may best utilize these observable gender patterns cannot be ascribed but emerge from the members, the issues raised, and group process it-self.

## Dimension Six: Power/Assertiveness

A central dimension of groupwork with differential gender expres-sion is that of assertiveness/power. The structure of group may reflect the inequities of society, which can disempower and even oppress women (Burden and Gottlieb, 1987; Hulse, 1985). Women may view their position in group as "weaker," and, therefore, may be less likely to assert themselves (Burden and Gottlieb, 1987). Men who have been more socialized to aggressively assert themselves, often in hier-archical one-up systems, are more able to assert themselves in rela-tion to others. In contrast women tend to internalize the assertion of power as a "less than feminine" quality, and are less willing to use it openly. It has been suggested that there may be a further gender divi-sion along the type and context of power; however, this issue remains unclear.

The dimension of "power/assertiveness" is closely related to the gender pattern dimensions of relational and communicative styles described above. The implications for practice emerge from the members group discussion, topics explored, communication, and in the group process. Facilitators need to be able to comment on the power/assertiveness of one or all of the group members in the mo-ment, often reflecting back or reframing verbal or nonverbal dynam-ics and interactions. This reflection of observable power-based pat-terns (such as hierarchy, power's quieting influence on women, or the enabling of men to engage assertively) can be effectively used to widen the issues or moment for the group members; or to challenge members' perspectives, recognition of others, or development of new thoughts. There can be no applied script in this dimension; rather, a facilitator's awareness of this gender pattern can open up unique and valuable intervention, which can foster interpersonal and intra-personal exploration.

## Dimension Seven: Self-Disclosure

Participant self-disclosure in group therapy has consistently received a great deal of attention. There are a myriad of constructs and dimensions concerning self-disclosure in the group structure and process. However, across theoretical orientations and group modalities, self-disclosure is considered a fundamental and essential component of group interaction (Corey and Corey, 1992; Brown, 1991; Rose, 1989; Yalom, 1985). According to Dolgin, Meyer, and Schwartz (1991), men relate more through activities than the emotional experience readily shared by women. Also, women are more likely to expect growth and comfort through the disclosure of feelings. Men, through socialization, view the expression of affect as difficult, weak, feminine, or often unacceptable (Kunkle and Gerrity, 1997; Brooks, 1996; Dolgin, Meyer, and Schwartz, 1991; Yalom, 1985). Expectations and responses by men and women toward self-disclosure may add pressure on members to disclose, which can adversely affect either gender (Schoener and Luepkner, 1996; Lakin, 1991).

Kunkle and Gerrity recognized that "self-disclosure is the fundamental means of group interaction" with important implications for practice (1997, p. 214). Although diminishing, the differing gender patterns regarding the dimension of self-disclosure have distinct implications for practitioners in groupwork. Group facilitators can readily enrich the group experience by encouraging members to discuss comfort level in disclosing or hearing the disclosures of others. If some members want to disclose but have difficulty, would they rather have others more willing to disclose first? Conversely, is it acceptable in group for a member not to disclose even when others do so? This dimension can have an enriching or a destructive impact on both individuals and the group as a whole. Sensitivity to this issue and awareness of its potential patterns are necessary characteristics for group facilitators.

## Dimension Eight: Anger

The last dimensions of gender diversity to be explored focus on two key affects that are frequently developed, displayed, responded to, and observed within group therapy. A significant male/female difference that tends to emerge during the group process is the emotion of anger. It has been consistently cited that the expression of anger is acceptable to men, often more so than the expression of any other emotion (Golden, 1997; Wright, 1994). Furthermore, anger in group can become the vehicle that men use to tap into and express other emotions less acceptable to males. The expression of anger for women, many authors have reflected, has been silenced by various cultural and social beliefs (Ewashen, 1997; Lazerson, 1992). It has been further suggested that women's anger may be related to suppression and repression (Ewashen, 1997; Munhall, 1993). Thereby, for women, anger is seen as unacceptable and can lead to withdrawal from the group process and from interpersonal interaction.

Anger, as identified earlier, appears to have a more delineated differential in relation to gender-patterned responses than the other dimensions do. The implications for practice along this dimension can have wider consequences. Since group treatment can often be affectively laden, and anger is recognized as the most acceptable of emotions expressed by men, this potential mix necessitates understanding. Group facilitators will inevitably be more able to work with group members, processes, and interpersonal interaction with enhanced awareness regarding gendered patterns of anger. It has been suggested that openly discussing the safety of the group to receive and contain difficult emotions, such as anger or shame, creates both an awareness and a preparation for members to address this issue in group and in themselves as it emerges during the treatment process. This can reduce the silencing of women when either their own anger or the anger of men emerges in the group process. Also, a group facilitator can utilize the clinical observable patterns by describing them to the group and processing their responses when anger develops in group. Again, it is important that the group facilitator recognize that these are patterns and are subject to change with every participant and group session.

### Dimension Nine: Shame

The final dimension to be explored is the powerful affect of shame. According to Wright (1994), males and females are trained by socialization into scripted roles, and if the role is not "played" properly, shame emerges. He further describes that men and women feel, experience, and respond to shame in differing ways. Men correlate shame with inadequacy, and they respond through attack or withdrawal in relation to this affect (Catherall and Shelton, 1996; Krugman, 1995; Wright, 1994). Women tend to cope with shame through depression (Wright, 1994; Osherson, 1992). However, women are often more able to process this affect because of their openness to expressing feelings and communicating with others. Also, both men and women often perceive and interpret shame as a sense of unworthiness.

Like anger, shame and the responses to it have both the potential for therapeutic curative effects or destructive outcomes. This is especially relevant as the noted clinical pattern response of males can evoke withdrawal or aggression. Group dynamics along this dimension may be further exacerbated because women seem to be somewhat more able to cope with shame and their responses to it.

A group facilitator who is aware of gendered responses regarding shame, like anger, may be better able to contain the potential harm of this affect while promoting its opportunity to enrich the group process and individual experiences. This often requires the facilitator to initially discuss and relate this issue to the group and recognize the potential for males and females to respond to this emotion as it may emerge or develop in group. Furthermore, as with anger, group facilitators can use the group processes to challenge and deconstruct, with members and each other, how individuals respond, internalize, understand, and effectively cope with shame. This also encourages the normalization of this emotion and the recognition of its potential effect on each of us. Also, coping with shame can aid in moving beyond the affect itself to the issue that provoked it.

## *GROUP AWARENESS*
## *OF GENDER DIVERSITY*

The group facilitator's awareness that observable gender patterns, not stereotypes or a negation of individual differences, exist will offer a myriad of implications for practice. The earlier discussions regarding the implications for practice address general conceptualizations for enriching application and are not designed as concrete, formalistic, or subject to specific differences.

An ongoing implication and available application for the enrichment of individuals and the group throughout the various group processes and stages is open awareness that gender diversity can affect the group. If the issue is raised without judgment, politics, or inherent value, the potential impact can enrich the group through a number of factors. First, the issue becomes open and available to discuss directly as required or needed. Second, the group can become a safe and open environment to discuss potentially difficult or delicate topics, concern, fears, or insecurities. Third, participants may become more aware of similarities, and thereby receive a sense of normalization. Fourth, individuals can witness that being candid and open about difficult issues can often facilitate healthy discussion and dissipate misconceptions or perceptions. Last, group members may recognize in themselves and in their circumstances and issues some of the effects of culture and socialization.

## CONCLUSION

Individuality is not constrained by patterns, typologies, archetypes, or stereotypes. Each individual and group of individuals contain intrinsically unique variations that affect, alter, and can move them beyond the norm. The homogeneous nature of gender is no different. However, observable patterns frequently reveal commonalities or tendencies that may be indicative of a specific group. Awareness of these similarities can be employed to enhance the group process.

Gender diversity in small groupwork has been shown to have a number of dimensions in which correlation can be observed to exist in patterned male/female responses. These clinically observable patterns have been demonstrated in both behavior and the expression of affect. These dimensions are merely patterned responses and not highlighted to contain judgment or effect gender equality in any way. Their existence offers a potentially enriching tool for group facilitators to enhance each individual's experience within a small group, and the group processes itself. Therapists, leaders, clinicians, and facilitators who work with individuals in groups can positively explore and utilize gender differences. It is hoped that greater study, implications for practice, and research of clinically observable patterns within gender diversity may continue and develop as an enriching tool for groupwork.

Pollack, W.S. (1995). No Man Is an Island: Toward a New Psychoanalytic Psychology of Men. In Levant, R.S. and Pollack, W.S. (Eds.), *A New Psychology of Men* (pp. 33-67). New York: Basic Books.

Pollack, W.S. (1998). *Real Boys: Rescuing Our Sons from the Myths of Boyhood.* New York: Henry Holt and Company.

Raubolt, R.R. and Rachman, A.W. (1995). A Therapeutic Group Experience for Fathers. In F. J. Turner (Ed.), *Differential Diagnosis and Treatment in Social Work* (Fourth Edition) (pp. 871-878). New York: The Free Press.

Roesler, T.A. and Lillie, B.K. (1995). Slaying the Dragon: The Use of Male/Female Co-Therapists for Adult Survivor Group Therapy. *Journal of Child Sexual Abuse 4*(2):1-17.

Rose, S.D. (1989). *Working with Adults in Groups: Integrating Cognitive-Behavioral and Small Group Strategies.* San Francisco: Jossey-Bass.

Rutan, J.S. and Stone, W.N. (1993). *Psychodynamic Group Psychotherapy* (Second Edition). New York: The Guilford Press.

Schoener, G.R. and Luepkner, E.T. (1996). Boundaries in Group Therapy: Ethical and Practical Issues. In DeChant, B. (Ed.), *Women and Group Psychotherapy: Theory and Practice* (pp. 373-399). New York: The Guilford Press.

Schubert-Walker, L.J. (1987). Women's Groups are Different. In Brody, C.M. (Ed.), *Women's Therapy Groups: Paradigms of Feminist Treatment* (pp. 3-12). New York: Springer Publishing Company.

Shaw, J.B. and Barrett-Power, E. (1998). The Effects of Diversity on Small Work Group Processes and Performance. *Human Relations 51*(10):1307-1325.

Shulman, L. (1992). *The Skills of Helping: Individuals, Families, and Groups* (Fouth Edition). Itasca, IL: F.E. Peacock Publishers, Inc.

Silverberg, R.A. (1986). *Psychotherapy with Men: Transcending the Masculine Mystique.* Springfield, IL: Charles C Thomas.

Sternbach, J. (1990). The Men's Seminar: An Educational and Support Group for Men. *Social Work with Groups 13*(2):23-39.

Tannen, D. (1990). *You Just Don't Understand: Women and Men in Conversation.* New York: William Morris.

Wallach, T. (1994). Competition and Gender in Group Therapy. *Group 18*(1):29-37.

Weinman, S. (1995). Male Therapist, Male Client—Conversations About Gender. *EAPisode, The Newsletter of the Employee Assistance Program Association of Toronto,* Spring, pp. 4-6.

White, M. (1995). *Re-Authoring Lives: Interviews and Essays.* Adelaide, South Australia: Dulwich Centre Publications.

White, M. and Epston, D. (1990). *Narrative Means to Therapeutic Ends.* New York: W.W. Norton.

Wilbur, M.P. and Roberts-Wilbur, J. (1994). Groupwork with Men's Beliefs. *The Journal for Specialists in Groupwork 19*(2):65-82.

Wright, F. (1994). Men, Shame, and Group Psychotherapy. *Group 18*(4):212-224.

Wright, F. and Gould, L.J. (1996). Research on Gender-Linked Aspects of Group Behavior: Implications for Group Psychotherapy. In DeChant, B. (Ed.), *Women and Group Psychotherapy: Theory and Practice* (pp. 333-350). New York: The Guilford Press.

Yalom, I.D. (1985). *The Theory and Practice of Group Psychotherapy* (Third Edition). New York: Basic Books.

Yalom, I.D. (1998). *The Yalom Reader.* New York: Basic Books.

Chapter 7

# Group Work with Minority Mentally Ill Men: The Role of the Woman Worker

Carol S. Hinote

This chapter describes three weekly groups, each engaging about five men in verbal and visual-artistic activities, that were led by this writer ("the worker") over a three-year period in a New York City medical center's mental health clinic. These were a support group for men thirty to forty-five years of age with mixed diagnoses and two groups for younger men diagnosed with psychotic disorder. As the largest outpatient unit of the medical center's psychiatry department, the clinic's multidisciplinary staff provided psychotherapy, assessment, and medication services to about 850 locally residing people of all age groups other than infancy. Nearly the entire population served by the clinic was poor and nonwhite, and nearly half were male. The served population's ethnic composition was roughly the same as that of the three weekly groups: about half African American, a quarter black Caribbean, and a quarter Latino. In contrast, nearly the entire professional staff at the clinic, including the worker, were white/non-Latino. The men in these groups had all been admitted to the clinic following a process of assessments, and nearly all were in medication (psychopharmacotherapy) programs while being seen by the worker for group therapy.

After stating the rationale and purpose for these groups, the chapter explores four important areas of concern:

- The role of the woman worker in leading men's groups
- The role of the white worker in leading nonwhite groups

- Men's resistance to discussing certain topics in groups
- Supervision of women workers who lead men's groups

## THE GROUPS' RATIONALE AND PURPOSE

The worker chose to lead men's groups to meet an increasing need she perceived for men in the clinic's served population to learn how to build support networks—that is, enduring relationships with people who care about and are helpful to them, and whom they care about and to whom they are helpful in return. The worker told the men of each group that she hoped to help them build friendships because that was something she was good at doing. The men's positive response reflected how much they felt unable to develop friendships and to gain peer and community acceptance due to their histories of stigmatization as "mentally ill," as well as their respective socialization deficits.

In many cases, these men had been referred to the clinic because their behavior had been perceived as putting themselves or others at risk of harm. Their treatment plans were formed with the assumption that changing their violent or threatening behavior patterns would require changing their belief systems and their patterns of affective experience (Stein, 1983). Hence, another goal set for the group work was for these men to sustain an acceptably low risk of reexhibiting inappropriate, aggressive, or violent behavior. The worker soon concluded that to reach this goal through addressing the beliefs and affective experiences that predisposed the men to problematic behavior, she should first address the beliefs and affective experiences that clashed with the idea that she or any other woman worker might be helpful to them.

The worker explained to each group that one of its chief purposes, not inconsistent with the goal of ending the members' predispositions to inappropriate, aggressive, or violent behavior, was "to help members promote caring and friendship between men." She was mindful of Stein's suggestion that "[b]reaking barriers to communication which present themselves as masculine patterns of relating to other people appears to be the most satisfying experience reported by the men who have participated in men's groups" (p. 155). The worker suggested to these men that, typically, women differ from men in their style of communication, and that this different style often proved more conducive to forming support networks and perhaps accounted for her own proficiency as a communicator. The men appeared to find the suggestion plausible and identified improvement of communication skills as an important goal of their work with her.

## THE ROLE OF THE WOMAN WORKER
## IN LEADING MEN'S GROUPS

In a society that conditions women to defer to men, to let them broker power (Bernardez, 1983), how does a woman become an effective leader of a group of men who are inclined to believe in stereotypes of women such as the "vengeful mother" and the "idealized mother" (Chodorow and Contratto, 1982)? Somehow the men must accept both her authority and her desire to help without reacting to her as either the vengeful mother who demands, goads, drives, withholds, and punishes, or the idealized mother who lacks personal needs, exists only for others, totally and unconditionally accepts others, lacks aggression, is never critical, and is always nurturing. "Providing structure and direction requires that the group worker be the acknowledged authority" (Kurland and Salmon, 1993, p. 153), yet the woman worker who assumes authority over men conflicts with cultural messages about women that the men have internalized throughout their lives. Bernardez says that the "female authority models who appear to meet the test with more success are those who are capable of firm benevolence: not bothered by the aggression and who can protect themselves from it and are capable of greater detachment, neutrality and objectivity" (p. 47).

The worker found such firm benevolence to be especially helpful in working with the younger psychotic men's groups, whose members joined directly following psychiatric hospitalizations. Early in their experience with the groups, these young men typically were barely stabilized on medication, were struggling to resettle in their homes and communities, and resented perceived efforts to control and manage them. For example, in his first session, Keith was hostile and threatening to the worker and other group members. As was her custom with all three groups, the worker had positioned herself closest to the door that allowed egress from the therapy room. When Keith's threatening behavior escalated, she opened the door, and Keith briefly calmed down. Later in the session, the worker responded to a reescalation by summoning her supervisor, who arranged for two security guards to stand just beyond the door for the remainder of the session. It took a few more sessions for Keith to show he could sustain an acceptable level of calm and stability in the group, and for the other members to curtail their fear of him. Eventually, Keith sustained a gentle manner, and the others enjoyed his presence.

Since most of the others had exhibited or witnessed inappropriate and frightening behavior like that Keith had shown, it was crucial for that group's members to conclude, as they did, that the worker would act to limit and gradually eliminate any such behavior without herself becoming angry or violent, and for them to see how they might act likewise. The day came when a new angry and hostile member was added to the same group, and Keith responded by telling this newcomer about his own troubled beginning and how much progress he had made since then.

In leading men's groups, the woman worker must manage her own anxiety and fear in tense situations, and present herself as caring but firm, despite any feelings of inadequacy in handling men's issues or any challenges from men who are primed to dread vengeful mothers or take advantage of idealized mothers. Firm benevolence helps to alleviate "the anger that can be an unconscious attempt to silence expected negative judgment" (Bernardez, p. 48). The worker has to ride out any storms calmly but with clear messages, both verbal and nonverbal, that she is in charge, that the group is safe, and that the group can contain the anger of struggling members. She should be willing to educate the group from the get-go about gender-related dynamics (Reed, 1983).

The worker did ask the men how they felt about having a woman worker as their leader. At first, they denied that it mattered. But subsequent discussions showed that it mattered a great deal. The men admitted that they felt a woman worker would be more nurturing and indicated that they would not trust a man, especially a white man, as their group leader. Their belief that a woman worker would be less powerful than a worker who was a man actually was comforting to them in the early stages. Nine of the fifteen members of the three groups lived with their mothers and were used to being taken care of and punished by women in positions of authority. In taking the lead of a men's group, the woman worker faces the problem of some men being inclined to reenact with her their struggles with mothers who have been vengeful or idealized. The woman worker can usually resolve this problem over time by providing consistent structure and encouraging men who show such inclinations to discuss their feelings about their mothers and other women, or to at least reveal those feelings in doing artwork.

Gambrill and Richey make the point that "lower status males behave with higher status males the way women behave with men" (1983, p. 53). So how do lower status males, minorities in this case, behave with women who are also seen as having less status? Interestingly, this position of lower status created a commonality between the worker and the group members. When talking about oppression, members reported that they felt heard and understood by the worker. The worker was able to offer valuable information about consciousness-raising from the feminist movement in relation to culturally assigned roles and profiling. The worker was careful not to align with the members against the "white male other" but offered support and sparked hope that they could manage their lives more effectively and with greater satisfaction.

## THE ROLE OF THE WHITE WORKER IN LEADING NONWHITE GROUPS

Asked whether it mattered to them that their race or ethnicity was different from that of the worker, the men responded as they did when asked about the gender difference. At first, they denied that it mattered, but subsequent discussions revealed that her being white/non-Latino did matter. Raising the issue clearly at the outset of each group invited and set the stage for later discussions of racial difference.

Erikson (1968) suggested that social identity development requires resolution of intrapsychic conflict related to the following areas: gender, religion, age, occupation, political ideology, and sexual orientation. Erikson did not mention racial identity as an important part of social identity development, discounting the impact of racial identity on white Americans, though he did acknowledge that African Americans experience negative identity development within the culture. According to Helms (1994), ignoring the fact that "white privilege" is an important part of white identity diminishes the understanding of difference, that of privilege and/or disadvantage among the races (p. 287). Helms adds that, whereas African Americans are challenged to overcome racist negative evaluations and to develop a positive identity rooted in their own culture, whites need to recognize and abandon an internalized sense that they are more privileged and to develop a new nonracist identity. It is crucial that the white group worker, particularly in taking the lead of a group that includes non-whites, be especially sensitive to the risk that an internalized (unconscious) racist sense of privilege could affect her work. It is also crucial that the white worker who leads a nonwhite group be especially sensitive to the risk that members' negative experiences with whites or as victims of racism could affect their participation, such as through expressions of mistrust and negative transference. With respect to her own moods and emotions, as well as those of the group members before her, the white worker in such a role must also be careful to distinguish nonrealistic anxiety germane to racial difference from anxiety germane to racial difference that is based on actual experience and accurate information. Of course, this is especially important in working with people who are in treatment explicitly because of their presentations of paranoia or acute anxiety, as were many of these men.

"One's own conflicts, which may be multidetermined, can complicate the work because they provide a barrier to the careful thinking that is necessary," says Pinderhughes (1993, p. 68). How group members view the world of work provides a poignant example of how the worker needs to be constantly assessing her values and related judgments. Even though having a mental illness was a significant stigma in the lives of these men, not being employed and feeling unemployable struck the worker as even more damaging. The men seemed to apply the values of both white and their own nonwhite cultures in judging themselves harshly for not drawing a paycheck. While a few of these men were in utter denial of being mentally ill or having serious functional limitations, others seemed to have concluded that disability due to mental illness permanently foreclosed opportunities for them to have satisfying intimate relationships, adequate housing, or social acceptance. They seemed convinced that no woman would want them without a job and that they would have little value to their children (many of them were fathers) because they lacked money to give them. These men often described themselves as invisible in their families because they lacked an occupation.

The worker recognized that it would not have been helpful for her to try fostering in these men the staunch, rather driven midwestern work ethic with which she had been raised. She began questioning her own value system about the world of work and how it might be impacting her own well-being as well as her work with these groups. Being sensitive to these differences can be enriching for the group and the worker. For these men to find meaning in their lives that is not necessarily based on having an occupation was quite a challenge. The worker found reason to wonder whether the tendency in our society to define women in "relational" rather than "occupational" terms (Gambrill and Richey, p. 55) allowed the men to feel more comfortable discussing the issues pertinent to having marginal or fragmented work histories with her than they might have felt in discussing them with a man.

## MEN'S RESISTANCE TO DISCUSSING CERTAIN TOPICS IN GROUPS

A fruitful exercise for the group was to develop a list of questions about their mental illnesses. One group session was spent with the clinic director answering their questions, which included the following (in the words they agreed to use):

- What is paranoia? Is it related to suicide?
- Why do I stay by myself? Even as a child, I stayed by myself.
- What is the chronology of schizophrenia? Where do professionals get their information?
- What are the rights of people with mental illness related to financial assistance and medical care?
- What is clinical depression?
- How does drug and alcohol abuse affect my mental illness?
- Does smoking have any impact on my mental illness?

It was difficult for these men to understand what their respective mental illnesses (in the language of the diagnostic model applied to them) were thought to be, and how these psychological conditions factored in their life experiences. A sense of empowerment was gained in developing the questions and then putting them to an expert with a powerful status. Following the exercise, the men seemed less self-critical and were motivated to obtain more information of this kind. The session was used as a springboard to revising their treatment plans to be more specific about goals and objectives, such as in the areas of socialization, development of vocational skills, and further education.

Sexual issues and concerns often came up in these groups. Sammy did a provocative drawing one day alluding to his feelings about the effects on his sex drive that he attributed to his prescribed medication. The drawing graphically depicted his desire to engage in sexual intercourse. His pill bottles were drawn in a little bubble over his head, suggesting his inability to achieve an erection. When the other group members saw this piece, they discussed similar feelings about taking their medication. This was an important and common problem for these men. Whether or not medications actually were rendering any of them impotent, the manufacturers of some of these medications have acknowledged that their possible side effects include impotency. The worker encouraged the men to talk openly with their psychiatrists about this concern and to ask about alternative interventions. Other members questioned whether the medication did account for the reported impotency. This consideration, among other concerns about relationships with women, was often brought up in subsequent sessions.

The men engaged in exercises related to anger and violence from a workbook series, *Men's Work* (Kivel, 1993). The first task entailed asking the men to consider what it meant to "act like a man" (p. 3). Each group member listed the qualities he thought were involved in acting like a man, and then the group developed a composite list, as follows (in the words they agreed to use):

- Work—get a job.
- Be responsible, be respectful.
- Be compassionate, be kind.
- Be like a man—grow up.
- Have your own apartment—pay your bills.
- Behave in a proper manner.
- Take care of your children.
- Maintain stability.
- Have confidence.

The members were then challenged to reflect on how it felt to live in the "Act Like a Man" box and what it might be like to be freed from the box. In the next session, members did artwork related to the box metaphor. On their external surfaces, the boxes represented the stereotypical qualities indicated in the composite list, while the boxes' interiors were used to represent qualities of a "softer" and more vulnerable kind. The men were able to discuss this contrast and relate it to their own lives, including "out on the street" in their neighborhoods.

Another workbook task required the group members to reflect on when they first observed or experienced violence. The men began talking about incidents from childhood featuring themselves as the victims of violence. They did not refer to these experiences as child abuse, though from a legal and clinical standpoint that was generally what it had been. Instead, they talked about how they were "disciplined." (The worker did not insist on distinguishing between "child abuse" and "discipline," used as a verb to mean trying to train a child to exercise self-control.) The members were asked to choose words that they associated with being "beaten." They jointly developed the following list:

- Shame
- Pain
- Fear
- Anger
- Stress
- Anxiety
- Self-blame

Asked how their beatings in childhood were affecting them now, the men mentioned being self-disciplined, being "a nervous wreck," and being timid. Upon concluding this exercise, the worker saw no reason to lecture the men on what constituted child abuse nor on the problems adult survivors of child abuse are prone to experience. Instead, the open discussion of how "being disciplined" as children affected them as adults that ensued in subsequent sessions increased their insight into this aspect of their lives without forcing them to adopt the perspective of the worker's culture.

For another member who was dealing with anger management, an "anger time line" was created in the group. The length of the line depicted the man's lifespan to date, divided into equal segments representing intervals of years, with dots placed to designate events when he had felt extremely angry. These events included the time his father left home (when he was eight years old) and episodes of perpetrating violence at school. Some explanatory words were inserted as close as possible to each dot. Scanning across the time line thus provided a historical narrative of the man's experience with severe anger. To summarize, in the groups, members were able to ask questions and talk about their own experiences with anger. Talking about their anger—when it started, its consequences—seemed to make their anger more self-manageable. Much like the feminist consciousness-raising groups the worker had belonged to, these groups gave the men settings where they could examine their own and each others' lives with more neutrality and objectivity than would otherwise have been possible.

The worker struggled with the feeling that working with the men was actually a form of social control—that is, a process conducted in the interests of the institutions that dominate society rather than in the interests of these men. In the past few years, New York City has had several highly publicized incidents in which severely mentally ill people, noncompliant with their treatment programs or not in any, had harmed citizens without provocation. In reaction to these incidents, the state of New York enacted laws and may enact more laws with the general aim of giving judges greater authority to order treatment for the mentally ill, especially those with violent histories. The repeated messages put out by the institutions dominating society, at least in New York, are "Keep them under control" and "We are afraid of them." It was important for the worker to bear in mind a point made by Barbara and John Ehrenreich (1974), that "to analyze something as a system of social control—as a mechanism for creating or reinforcing acquiescence to the given order of society—is not to view it as a conspiracy" (p. 26). It was also important to remain focused on the rationale and purpose of these groups, and not to succumb to devaluing this work in response to cultural attitudes and mandates. In other words, the worker learned to trust each group's process and strength to naturally move toward fulfilling its purpose and goals for the benefit of its members. It helped to review the progress being made. For example:

- Keith, twenty-three, had avoided hospitalization for two years, was stable on medication, and in the past year had been taking college courses.
- Henry, forty, who had joined one of the groups while suffering severe panic attacks and agoraphobia that had begun after having a mild stroke, was taking public transportation regularly and had reduced the frequency of his panic attacks to just once or twice per month.
- Jason, thirty-three, who had been incarcerated from age fifteen to twenty-five and had come to the group, showing self-inflicted cigarette burns, at his mother's insistence because he was hearing voices and sleeping all day, had not engaged in self-mutilation for more than two years, and was attending and profiting from a daily psychiatric rehabilitation treatment program.
- Earl, forty-four, diagnosed as schizophrenic, had had many hospitalizations since his first psychotic break occurred when he was a twenty-year-old student at one of the nation's most prestigious universities, but he had had no hospitalizations in the past three years, was attending his group regularly, and was attached to and friendly with its members.

## SUPERVISION OF WOMEN WORKERS
## WHO LEAD MEN'S GROUPS

In this section of the chapter, the writer refers to herself as "the supervisor," for while leading the three groups, she supervised six other therapists plus several student interns who practiced in a number of psychiatric units at the medical center, including the units charged with outpatient alcohol treatment, inpatient drug/alcohol detoxification, inpatient twenty-eight-day drug/alcohol rehabilitation, outpatient intensive psychiatric rehabilitation treatment, long-term residential treatment for the persistently mentally ill, and outpatient mental health treatment. All the supervisees were women who during their supervision by the worker began to lead or colead men's groups. Through this experience as a supervisor, the worker found that "[a]s the therapist explores his or her personhood in relationship to the client, the supervisor should create an atmosphere for mutual trust and must use expertise, knowledge, and personal experience to help the therapist improve the quality of his or her skills" (Peterson, 1991, p. 27).

The supervisor observed that two members of a psychotic men's group she co-led with one of her supervisees, a woman intern in her twenties, were subjecting the supervisee to sexually provocative comments. In the first few weeks, the intern responded to such comments by abruptly changing the topic. In supervision, the supervisor asked the intern to describe her feelings about being subjected to these comments. The intern replied that she found them upsetting but felt that ignoring them would eventually lead the men in question to stop. The supervisor then asked whether there was anything the intern might be doing to encourage the comments. She became defensive, stating, "I am not doing anything." She was asked to think what she might do to stop the comments and to consider what type of clothing she wore on group days. At the next session of the group, the sexually provocative comments continued with silence from the intern. She had chosen to wear more conservative, looser, and less revealing clothing. Just after the session ended, she angrily told the supervisor that wearing different clothing did not help and asked that the supervisor intervene to stop the comments. Asked what she believed the supervisor should say to the group, she said, "Tell them to stop and that it is not OK to talk to me that way." The supervisor asked the intern to give the men that message herself, with the supervisor being available to give support. During the next session, with some difficulty, she did ask the two men to cease making the comments and stated how uncomfortable their comments made her feel. One of the other group members stated, "I wondered how long you were going to put up with it." The group as a whole was supportive and the comments never resumed.

In both individual and group supervision, it was apparent that these women workers had reservations about working with the populations that came to them. Initially, it was easy for these women to fall into the pattern of complaining about how difficult this population could be to engage and helped to move toward goals and objectives. To respond with effective remedies, the supervisor had to probe to find the basic reasons for their complaints. She generally found a combination of reasons, including feelings of inadequacy, fear, internalized cultural stereotypes, inexperience with being a leader, and, conversely, being accustomed to working with men in a role that was cooperative and supportive rather than authoritative. As a result of this exploration, the supervisor drafted this list of needs for preparing women workers to take the lead of men's groups.

- Training related to gender dynamics in groups
- Training in "cultural competency" and otherwise handling the issues of social diversity
- Help with understanding the dynamics of being a woman authority figure
- Group therapy training, including training in safety aspects and in otherwise handling group members' conflict and anger
- Supportive, consistent, and informed supervision

One of the most important transitions in the course of a worker's leadership of a group occurs when she is able to see conflict as a sign of health. "Because of their fears about conflict, when differences arise in a group students often ignore the problem-solving process and jump prematurely to 'solve' problems" (Kurland and Salmon, 1993, p. 88). Without guidance, workers often develop a "fix-it" attitude. The supervisor can help the worker slow the process down and place the responsibility for change back on the group members collectively and individually. If the group becomes a safe enough place for members to express conflict without aggression, yelling, making threats, or actual violence, they are making important progress that can be generalized into other settings in their lives. When the members know that the worker will provide structure and keep the group safe, the group can be an arena where new behaviors can be tested with support and feedback. The supervisor needs to nurture and guide the worker through this transition and help the worker to bind any related anxiety that she may experience. The supervisor needs to be the "good enough" other. The supervisor's role is key for women who want to take on the exciting challenge of working with troubled men.

## CONCLUSION: IMPLICATIONS FOR PRACTICE

If groups continue to be created on the basis of client need, many more men's groups will be formed in the future. With appropriate support and training, women workers can be valuable and effective leaders of men's groups. In a society that makes the conflicts and problems between the genders a subject of considerable attention, women who lead men's groups may themselves get much attention and perhaps credit for helping men escape their "Act Like a Man" boxes. Meanwhile, women who do clinical work with men need to become more comfortable as the firm, benevolent other. To generalize further, there is now a golden opportunity for therapists of one gender who work with people of the other to be in the vanguard of the effort to move society beyond ill-fitting, limiting, and destructive gender stereotypes. And group therapy may be the most appropriate modality in which therapists might pursue this golden opportunity.

# REFERENCES

Bernardez, T. (1983). "Women in authority: Psychodynamic and interactional aspects." In Reed, B.G. and Garvin, C.D. (Eds.), *Groupwork with Women/Groupwork with Men* (pp. 43-49). Binghamton, NY: The Haworth Press.

Chodorow, N. and Contratto, S. (1982). "The fantasy of the perfect mother." In Thorne, B. (Ed.), *Rethinking the Family* (pp. 54-75). New York: Longman.

Ehrenreich, B. and Ehrenreich, J. (1974). "Health care and social control." *Social Policy* 5(1).

Erikson, E. (1968). *Identity: Youth and Crisis*. New York: W.W. Norton.

Gambrill, E. and Richey, C. (1983). "Gender issues related to group social skills training," *Social Work with Groups, 6.*

Glover, B. (1983). "Women leaders in small groups: Social-psychological perspectives and strategies." *Social Work with Groups, 6.*

Helms, J. (1994). "The conceptualization of racial identity and other 'racial' constructs." In Trickett, E., Birman, D., and Watts, B. (Eds.), *Human Diversity: Perspectives on People in Context.* New York: Jossey-Bass.

Kivel, P. (1993). *Men's Work: Growing Up Male Identifying Violence in My Life.* Center City, MN: Hazelden Educational Materials.

Kurland, R. and Salmon, R. (1993). "Not just one of the gang: Group workers and their role as an authority." *Social Work with Groups, 16*(1/2).

Kurland, R. and Salmon, R. (1998). *Teaching a Methods Course in Social Work with Groups, Unit 8.* Alexandria, VA: Council on Social Work Education.

Peterson, F. (1991). "Issues of race and ethnicity in supervision: emphasizing who you are, not who you know." *Social Work with Groups, 14*(2).

Pinderhughes, E. (1993). *Understanding Race, Ethnicity, and Power: The Key to Efficacy in Clinical Practice.* London: The Free Press.

Reed, B.G. (1983). "Women leaders in small groups: Social-psychological perspectives and strategies." In Reed, B.G. and Garvin, C.D. (Eds.), *Groupwork with Women/Groupwork with Men* (pp. 33-42). Binghamton, NY: The Haworth Press.

Stein, T. (1983). "An overview of men's groups." *Social Work with Groups, 6.*

Chapter 8

# Building Bridges Over Troubled Waters: A Bridging Model for Teleconferencing Group Counselling

Sandra Regan

## *INTRODUCTION*

This chapter explores teleconferencing group counselling in terms of technical aspects, group work models, and interpersonal connections, which have in common bridging functions. The word "bridge" is used as a metaphor to help conceptualise what is happening in teleconferencing counselling groups.

How are teleconferencing groups connected? A teleconference bridge is the electronic device that connects all participants. It implies more than just a technical link. It represents the potential for the help that is available at the other end of the line. It connects people dispersed over wide geographic areas, creating a group that would otherwise not exist. It provides the link for the lonely, the isolated, and those unable to access services or who do not see face-to-face groups as their choice modality. Technically, it provides the means to build interpersonal bridges, which would not have been possible without use of this electronic device.

Just as one recognises the role of technology in teleconferencing group counselling, one must also recognise that conceptual bridges must be crossed in order to create new ways of working with groups. The changing context creates new challenges, and one must look at how face-to-face group work models can be adapted. The variety of theoretical models used in face-to-face social group work (see Brown, 1991, pp. 38-41) cannot necessarily be used in the same way within teleconferencing group counselling.

The expressed intent of teleconferencing group counselling, in most circumstances, is for therapeutic purposes, which must be acknowledged by the leader and the participants before the group begins. The same group work principles and ethics are used as in face-to-face counselling groups, and thus one needs to be able to articulate the specific theoretical framework upon which interventions are based.

Teleconferencing group counselling, as explored in this chapter, has a time-limited format: participants meet for a specified period of time over a prescribed number of sessions. The therapeutic focus engages people experiencing problems in specific areas of their life, whether these are personal, relationship, or practical aspects, and thus helps people to cope with the current situation. It also offers the opportunity for participants to handle similar situations in a more beneficial way in the future.

In leading teleconferencing counselling groups since 1992, I have worked with populations as diverse as people with vision impairments, families of organ donors, and former caregivers of people with Alzheimer's (Regan, 1992; 1997; 1997-1998). Briefly, the groups were all run under agency auspices and attracted funding. Members came to the groups through referrals from within agencies. In terms of member composition, teleconferencing seemed to allow for a wider range of diversity in demographic characteristics, perhaps due to lack of visual cues. The most important composition factor was members' common struggle with a specific challenge. Dates and times of meetings were based on members' needs, with groups being run both day and evening. In most instances, eight one-hour sessions over consecutive weeks was found to be a sufficient time frame to accomplish counselling objectives. The size of the groups varied from four to six members with two coleaders.

It is hoped that this chapter will encourage others working in the area of telephone group work to develop teleconferencing models (see Schopler, Galinsky, and Abell, 1997; Schopler, Abell, and Galinsky, 1998).

## TELECONFERENCING BRIDGING MODEL (TBM)

The TBM presented in this chapter should be looked at as a transitional model, a first attempt to pull together experiences and thus a work in progress. It provides a bridge from working with face-to-face groups to teleconferencing group counselling and an awareness of some of the changes that need to occur along the way to utilise the medium of teleconferencing to advantage.

The TBM integrates aspects of theme-centred interactional (Cohn, 1972; Shaffer and Galinsky, 1974; Anderson, 1984) and interactional mutual aid (Schwartz, 1961; Shulman, 1992) models of group work, specifically relating them to teleconferencing group counselling. Just as a group is more than the sum of its parts, aspects of these two models together create a synergy that is quite different from each model used separately. Components that can be integrated from the theme-centred interactional model include the "I," "We," "It," and the "Globe," and the dynamics of mutual aid from the interactional mutual aid model.

Both models, theme centred interactional and interactional mutual aid, emphasise individuals reaching out and connecting with others in order to grow. They focus on both process and content. This author sees the theme-centred interactional model emphasising *content*— that is, the focus is on the problem or theme to be dealt with. The mutual aid model, however, emphasises more strongly the *process* to be achieved within a teleconference hookup. It is important not to confuse the process of mutual aid, as discussed in this chapter, with group process in general, which occurs in both models.

Schwartz (1961) made a helpful observation when referring to face-to-face groups which holds true for teleconferencing counselling groups.

> The group is an enterprise in mutual aid, an alliance of individuals who need each other, in varying degrees, to work on certain common problems. The important fact is that this is a helping system in which the clients need each other as well as the worker. This need to use each other, to create not one but many helping relationships is *a vital ingredient of the group process and constitutes a common need over and above the specific task for which the group was formed.* (sic) (18)

Thus, mutual aid is just one ingredient of group process. It does not include all of group process. Schwartz's common need, which emphasises mutual aid, demonstrates the kind of emphasis I place on the process of mutual aid in teleconferencing group counselling.

This may appear to be a simplified approach, but the content or theme stands out in the theme-centred interactional model, whereas the process of mutual aid is predominant in the interactional mutual aid model. The objective of this chapter is not to present a totally new model but to look at what aspects of these two face-to-face group work models can be integrated to create a meaningful teleconferencing bridging model.

## *THEME-CENTRED INTERACTIONAL MODEL*

The theme-centred interactional model (Cohn, 1972: Shaffer and Galinsky, 1974; Anderson, 1984), with its focus on content, provides a base from which to discuss how it facilitates teleconferencing group counselling and its role in TBM.

The theme-centred interactional model has a focus on content because it utilises themes as a way of moving the group forward. Although it also considers group process, it is always in relation to the theme. Even the name of the model gives the impression that the theme has particular significance. One becomes aware of content first, then process.

The theme-centred interactional model consists of four distinct parts: the "I," "We," "It," and the "Globe." These are in constant interaction and may change from one moment to the next. The "Globe" represents the environment of the group. The "I" represents individual contributions to the group. The "We," group interactions creating group process. The "It" is the content reflected in an overall theme and subthemes (Shaffer and Galinsky, 1974). Although explicit attention is given to each, the theme or "It" has inherent priority.

The leader's role is to maintain a balance between the three components "I-We-It" within the parameters of the "Globe." The group goes through highs and lows, reflecting tensions between the three components. Problems arise when too much emphasis is given to one part at the expense of the other two over a long period. This detracts from the other two and works against proper theme development (Shaffer and Galinsky, 1974). Each component is present to some degree, but the theme or "It" is always ready to reassert. Theme development requires all three, yet in reality the theme seems to dominate.

The theme-centred interactional model provides structure by setting a clear-cut overall theme and subthemes for each session, focusing group interaction without being coercive (Shaffer and Galinsky, 1974). Structure seems imperative in teleconferencing when members cannot see each other and therefore do not have access to non-verbal communication. Without structure, there is a tendency for teleconferencing groups to become aimless and wander from one topic to another.

The adoption of an overall theme and subthemes also provides efficiency and time limits for the group. Contact is usually for one hour. The theme establishes clear boundaries which help to keep the group on track.

Specific subthemes are introduced at the beginning of each teleconferencing session, creating the ensuing focus. Subthemes must relate to the overall theme but are more specific and task-oriented. They must be broad enough to allow a variety of member responses, yet narrow enough to create meaningful interactions. Although subthemes provide structure, the model also allows for change to meet participants' needs.

Subthemes are designed to capitalise on specific phases of group development. Thus, the first subtheme is used to establish common ground, but each successive subtheme is more demanding of individuals and the group. As the level of awareness and emotional content gradually increase, there needs to be a fit between the content and the group process.

The theme-centred interactional model helps to deal with sudden beginnings and endings. These beginnings and endings are unlike face-to-face groups because there is no time for gradually connecting or slowly disengaging, as with face-to-face groups. In teleconferencing group counselling, individuals are linked with other group members in an instant. A process of connection needs to begin immediately. The overall theme and subthemes help provide common ground and begin the process of connection, which eventually overlaps with the process of mutual aid. The subtheme helps the group to begin and also helps the group to end. There is no opportunity for a slow disengagement. One is connected with others and then all of a sudden alone.

During the last fifteen minutes, the teleconferencing group revisits the subtheme of the session, looking at lessons learned from the past and possible new strategies to work on challenges. This alerts members that the session will shortly be coming to an end and helps the group to wind down. At the end, the leader gives the subtheme for the next session.

The "Globe" creates an outer boundary which, in addition to general environment concerns, includes telephone, personal, and agency environments. The telephone environment includes the electronic bridge which connects members, participants' degree of comfort in using the telephone, and the technological problems that might occur.

The personal environment is where members receive their teleconference call. It is their territory and in most instances is familiar and nonthreatening. This differs from a face-to-face group with everyone in the same location. However, as with face-to-face groups, the personal environment also refers to personal situations and, in most instances, why people are in the group.

The agency, which organises the teleconference, constitutes the agency environment. The range of teleconferencing counselling groups may be limited according to agency functions and the use of technology.

## INTERACTIONAL MUTUAL AID MODEL

What roles does the interactional mutual aid model play in teleconferencing group counselling and TBM? The interactional mutual aid model emphasises process more because it focuses on the way the group operates. Mutual aid is the process by which the group connects to achieve its objectives. Content is always considered within the context of mutual aid, but mutual aid is the means to an end. It is the unifying concept that permeates the entire model.

The dynamics of mutual aid are common to both face-to-face groups and teleconferencing group counselling but with some differences in emphasis. These dynamics include: sharing data, the dialectical process, discussing taboo areas, the all-in-the-same-boat phenomenon, developing a universal perspective, mutual support, mutual demand, individual problem solving, rehearsal, and the strength-in-numbers phenomenon (Shulman, 1992, pp. 275-281).

Shulman points out that the potential for mutual aid exists in face-to-face groups, but simply bringing people together does not guarantee that such aid emerges. The same can be said about teleconferencing counselling groups. Merely connecting people through a teleconferencing bridge does not guarantee that mutual aid will occur.

Some may think the lack of nonverbal cues inhibits mutual aid. This may create an extra burden for group leaders because until people become more familiar with teleconferencing group counselling, they may be placed in the position of proving that a mutual aid process can be created in such a group. Yet the lack of nonverbal cues may contribute to the strength of mutual aid because the very strong verbal network may result in more reaching out as a consequence. Not only can a mutual aid process be created, the other elements of group process such as norms, roles, cohesion, communication patterns, as well as stages of group development are recognisable.

The concept of mutual aid takes on different dimensions in teleconferencing group counselling. The teleconferencing bridge that links participants may appear to be fragile, but its power lies in its use. Partly because members cannot see each other, they seem to invest more in the process of mutual aid, thus providing a comfort zone, while at the same time providing the strength and support needed to tackle difficult issues. Given the importance of the mutual aid system, the more quickly mutual aid dynamics can be established, the better it is for the group.

Teleconferencing group counselling provides an intense sense of connection for group members, which can be surprising. Even in a first session, quick rapport may occur. Early self-disclosures, which may be perceived as inappropriate in face-to-face groups, seem an acceptable part of the general group process.

As a teleconferencing counselling group develops, the dynamics of mutual aid (Shulman, 1992) become apparent but also some variations result due to the teleconferencing medium. Each dynamic will be looked at separately, highlighting the differences due to teleconferencing. Teleconferencing opens up opportunities for like-minded people who may be unable to attend face-to-face counselling groups to *share data*. Sharing data seems to occur more quickly. Perhaps because participants are aware of time limits or have held in their thoughts and feelings for so long, they seem more than ready to talk when the opportunity presents itself.

The lack of opportunity to attend face-to-face groups means that many participants have not had the chance to engage in a *dialectical process* and challenge their ideas with others going through a similar experience. Teleconferencing group counselling provides this opportunity. As the worker strives to find the elements of common ground, members become aware of other possibilities for change and ways to move forward.

Anonymity seems to encourage the *discussion of taboo areas.* Taking risks is easier if others' nonverbal communications cannot be seen. Embarrassment or discomfort, unless betrayed by tone of voice, remain invisible. In contrast, a face-to-face group may sometimes stop people before they get a chance to begin. Mutual aid develops to support disclosures.

Members are often surprised to find other people like themselves who experience similar thoughts and feelings. Sharing seems to make these thoughts and feelings a little less ominous. The "all-in-the-same-boat" phenomenon and the "all-on-the-same-telephone-line" connection strengthens the common bond, which contributes to the mutual aid system. Within this context, *developing a universal perspective* may also help lift the burden of self-blame. Because many participants live in rural or remote areas or in isolation, they are unable to achieve this sharing through face-to-face groups. Even those who live in urban areas may be isolated with no opportunity to share.

Providing *mutual support* encourages deeper explorations. Support is just a phone call away. Members recognise that support can be provided over the telephone and that collective mutual aid is quite different in strength from a one-to-one telephone conversation.

Participants need to move beyond understanding and caring to mutual demand. *Mutual demand* implies action. This is particularly important in a time-limited group. The leader initially makes the demand for work, but the most effective demands for work come from fellow group members. Because they are coming from the same experience zone and have earned the right to confront, they may do so in ways not open to the leader. Sometimes it is easier to make mutual demands over the telephone than face-to-face. The strength of mutual aid may also result in members being more motivated to do something for which they have the support of the teleconferencing group. Returning to the group to report success or failure, they know the group will accept them. Members may want to tackle problems but not know how to begin, perhaps avoiding difficult material. It would be easier to ignore the difficult material, but mutual demand enables its expression.

By focusing on participants' problems and working together as a group, *individual problem solving* can occur. Many ideas provide opportunities for different solutions and options for resolution compared with working alone. The distance barriers overcome by teleconferencing may also suggest different ways of handling things and different services based on geographical location. *Rehearsal* takes the form of mini role-plays, which allow members to explore and try out approaches to different situations via teleconferencing.

The support of others and the willingness to act together can increase the number of potential resolutions. This is demonstrated by the *strength-in-numbers* phenomenon. This is especially true if the group wants to improve services in their particular problem area. Without teleconferencing, their opportunities to experience this strength may be limited.

## STRUCTURE OF THE TELECONFERENCING BRIDGING MODEL

The TBM recognises the need to build bridges to a wider range of group members. Teleconferencing reaches those who have many times been denied access to services. These members in turn might form or maintain their own bridges after the group. Themes ensure that information and ideas are transferred across the bridge, and mutual aid maintains the bridge, thus traffic in ideas and themes can travel in both directions in the comfort of mutual aid. These two models are drawn together, creating a different conceptual understanding to maximise the use of teleconferencing. In TBM, both models are visible, but at specific times the parts merge, with the technology enabling the group to exist.

The theme-centred interactional model fills in the bridge span. It represents the content carried over the bridge and helps to make adjustments as one accesses and exits the bridge, while the mutual aid process provides the bridge supports or pylons.

The connection is made through a teleconferencing bridging system which connects individual telephone lines. These lines represent the roads to be travelled. One must assume the lines will be strong enough to carry one over the bridge even though they may appear quite fragile; in fact, they can carry the potential collective strength of the group.

A diagrammatic representation of the Teleconferencing Bridging Model is presented in Figure 8.1. The outer circle represents the "Globe" or group environment. This model operates in a general environment that all face-to-face as well as teleconferencing groups would recognise. However, within the group environment, specific variations are created or impacted on by the use of teleconferencing technology, and personal and agency environments. The telephone creates a specific environment that emphasises listening, not seeing. Because each member is in a different place, there are many personal environments. The agency environment has to take into account reactions that specifically relate to the use of technology. The "Globe" represents the outer boundary of this model, which in turn encompasses the mutual aid system.

The mutual aid system, as an ingredient of group process, provides a group environment as well as the common bond that connects the group. In many ways, mutual aid represents the essence of the group, what people remember, the intangible connection, what is retained but not seen or touched. The mutual aid system in turn encompasses the "I-We-It."

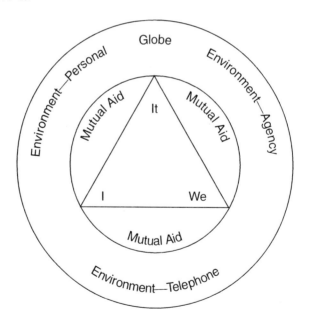

FIGURE 8.1. Teleconferencing Bridging Model

The "I-We-It" represents the inner workings of the group, including other general elements of group process, not the specifics of mutual aid. The "It" is at the apex of the triangle, and at some point the eye is drawn to it. The same is true in the group. Thus the inner-workings of the group support the content or theme through group process. All the boundaries are permeable with movement in both directions.

### What Makes the TBM Work?

What make these two models compatible in TBM? Both offer different things and yet complement each other. A group is more than the sum of its individual members, and TBM becomes more than just a sum of these two models, for together something quite different is created. With the lack of nonverbal communication, mutual aid becomes preeminent. It becomes even more important because it provides the base for interactions to occur. In a face-to-face group, one has additional nonverbal communication. The theme-centred interactional model's contribution is its capacity to exploit short periods of time constructively, when structure takes on added significance. It is also valuable because of the lack of nonverbal cues and the way it handles sudden beginnings and endings. Themes provide structure and security.

### CONCLUSION

A TBM of group work opens up opportunities for growth and change by which group members can develop interpersonal bridges as part of the helping process. They build bridges over troubled waters.

In TBM, the leader's role is to create an environment in which identified themes can be addressed and the mutual aid process facilitated. These are key elements in the helping process.

Finally, I have utilised both theme-centred interactional and interactional mutual aid models separately in teleconferencing group counselling. Each time I was left with the feeling that something was missing. In consequence, I have taken the salient points from each model and integrated them into a new transitional model. Having said this, there may well be many different approaches to teleconferencing group counselling, but at this point, TBM appears to be useful. This chapter presents an opportunity to share what works and why and to invite others to test the model.

## REFERENCES

Anderson, J. (1984). *Counseling through group process.* New York: Springer Publishing.

Brown, L.N. (1991). *Groups for growth and change.* New York: Longman Publishing.

Cohn, R. (1972). Style and spirit of the theme-centered interactional method. In Sager, C.J. and Kaplan, H.S. (Eds.), *Progress in group and family therapy* (pp. 857-858). New York: Brunner Mazel.

Regan, S. (1992). Theme-centred teleconferencing counselling groups: Working with vision-impaired elderly women. *Social Group Work Monograph,* Vol. III, University of New South Wales School of Social Work, Sydney, Australia: 2-13.

Regan, S. (1997). Overcoming the tyranny of distance: Exploring the use of teleconferencing group counselling. *Australian Social Work 50*(1):9-14.

Regan, S. (1997-1998). Teleconferencing group counselling: Pre-group public phase. *Groupwork 10*(1):5-20.

Schopler, J.H., Abell, M.D., and Galinsky (1998). Technology based groups: A review and conceptual framework for practice. *Social Work 43*(3):254-267.

Schopler, J.H., Galinsky, M.J., and Abell, M.D. (1997). Creating community through telephone and computer groups: Theoretical and practice perspectives. *Social Work with Groups 20*(4):19-34.

Schwartz, W. (1961). The social worker in the group. In *New perspectives on services to groups: Theory, organization and practice* (pp. 7-34). New York: National Association of Social Workers.

Shaffer, J.B. and Galinsky, M.D. (1974). The theme-centered interactional method. In *Models of group therapy and sensitivity training* (pp. 242-264). Englewood Cliffs, NJ: Prentice-Hall.

Shulman, L. (1992). *The skills of helping: Individuals, families, and groups* (Third edition). Itasca, IL: Peacock Publishers.

Chapter 9

# Groupworkers in the Making: A Simulation for Teaching Social Groupwork

Nancy Sullivan
Ellen Sue Mesbur

## *SIMULATION AS A CLASSROOM LEARNING TOOL*

The elements of learning process and content may be as central in a social groupwork course as are group process and content in a social work practice group. Because groupwork skills are an interactional application of knowledge and humanistic values, it makes sense to provide students with academic learning experiences in a "live action" mode. As stated by Kurland and Salmon (1998): "The classroom should be a place where students can struggle with ideas together . . . in a spirit of collegial cooperation" (p. 1).

The Bachelor of Social Work program at Ryerson Polytechnic University in Toronto is fortunate to have a roster of simulated clients available through the university's Interpersonal Skills Teaching Centre. Simulated clients (simulators) are individuals who have been trained to role-play specific client situations and to give detailed feedback to students. The client situations, or profiles, are fictitious, though created with knowledge of the field. The simulators are trained to portray one or more roles, to add or delete complicating variables, to increase or decrease the severity of the problem, and to represent various stages of the helping or problem-solving process from beginning to end (Wodarski and Kelly, 1987, as cited in Barsky et al., 1997).

Simulations provide learners with new and challenging experiences but at the same time protect them from some of the risks and anxieties associated with experiential learning in real practice. The environment of the simulation gives learners opportunities to process and generalize their learning at the time of the experience (Kenyon, 1995). One of the fundamental tasks of social work educators is to teach students how to apply theory to practice and how theories illuminate our practice decisions. While the task of learning about social groupwork theories may pose some challenges to students, a greater challenge is for them to learn the requisite skills of tuning in, assessing the group as a whole as well as each member, and working with the group as members struggle with the normal developmental issues of participating in a group (Papell, 1997). Group simulations offer students opportunities to work with a group and learn from feedback given by their peers, the instructor, and the simulators. The simulated group, with its practice challenges, presents a classroom learning experience for all the students together and provides "cognitive, interactive, and affective learning in a safe and controlled environment" (Kenyon, 1995, p. 179). The use of a simulated group can assist students in learning some basic social groupwork skills prior to working with groups, thus possibly avoiding inadequate practice with "real" group members by preparing them for the transition to actual practice.

Use of a simulated group in the classroom is a unique, collective, experiential learning opportunity. The richness of this peer engagement in professional education recognizes and "mines" the "golden" resources that lie within classroom membership. The learning process becomes a shared endeavour of students participating with the simulators, one another, and the instructor in a spirit of mutual support and enterprise. Since the simulators are believable in the roles they are playing, the learning atmosphere typically is charged with both nervous apprehension, an air of adventure, and eagerness to "test the theory."

Use of simulated clients in a particular class varies with the instructor's design and learning objectives for students. Usually, the simulators remain inconspicuously outside the classroom until the class is ready for the simulation to begin. They enter in role and stay in it until the entire simulation is finished. Only during the last twenty or thirty minutes of the class do they emerge from the role, introduce themselves, and proceed to give detailed feedback to each student social worker on his or her "practice." A number of students may be asked to volunteer to act as the five or six social group workers in following weeks' classes in the class prior to the simulation date to save time on the actual day and to allow those students to be ready. Once the simulation begins, the rest of the class, sitting in an arrangement for best viewing, observes in silence. The successive student workers choose to continue or begin again at their turn in acting as the social group worker with the simulated group.

At any time, the student worker or the instructor can call "time out" to stop the action. Often, when the student stops it, it is because she or he is stuck and requests input in order to proceed. The instructor may stop the action to make a teaching point or to assist in the student's intervention. Sometimes, instructors give the observing students the opportunity to call time-out to offer an idea that can't wait. During time-outs, the simulators sit motionless with heads down. Frequently, they use these moments to record their feedback notes for later.

## *GROUP SIMULATION EXAMPLE*

The simulation presented in this chapter, the "Chaotic Teen Group," consists of six multiethnic teenagers, four girls and two boys, all of whom are from families characterized by violence, turmoil, and uncertainty. Each of the teens has been at some time, and some are at present, in foster or alternate care. Their relationships with families, school, community, and peers are tenuous and tentative. These young people are at the threshold of adulthood and its responsibilities, but they are lacking solid nurturing and life-skills preparation. Their affect and behaviour are erratically inconsistent and unpredictable. Their fears and anxieties are palpable. Role profiles of the six group members are provided as an appendix to the chapter.

The Chaotic Teen Group Simulation was brought into the fourth class of Ryerson's one-semester Advanced Social Groupwork course for students in years three or four of their BSW program. Although upper-level students, they may have had, to date, no practice experience in working with a group in a social work role. The majority of them, though keen, were groupwork novices.

On the day of our simulation, three students played "the worker": Tanya, Manuel, and Amy. They all, especially Tanya who went first, deserve much credit for their willingness to try out their incipient skills in front of their peers, instructors, and a video camera. Acknowledging that working skillfully and successfully with a group requires a foundation of theory for practice, the following material, in the form of an enhanced process recording, illustrates some excerpts of practice when knowledge and skill base are those of fledgling social workers.

Excerpts 1, 2, and 3 are followed by feedback to the student worker from the simulators, to demonstrate the possible learning from those on the receiving end of the practice. Incorporated into the analysis sections on the students' interventions is teaching input from the instructors present at the simulation, to show how course content may be incorporated into an experiential learning activity and how "coaching" the student workers may prepare them for their next steps. Incorporated also are constructive and supportive comments from peers in the class during the time-out periods, a third means of learning the applied theory of social groupwork. The fourth sphere of learning possible with a simulation, personal learning on the part of student workers, is assumed to occur throughout the entire simulation, and in some spots is visible when the same student worker continues after a time-out.

### Excerpt #1: Student Social Worker Tanya

TANYA: OK, are we ready to start? (Pause.) Do you think? I thought we'd go around one more time and we could tell everybody our names . . . I'll start. I'm Tanya. (no smile; flat expression, but is scanning the group) And . . . (looks at Kali) do you want to go next?

KALI: I'm Kali.

TANYA: Hi, Kali.

LUREEN: I'm Lureen.

TANYA: Loreen?

LUREEN: Lureen.

JASMINE: Jasmine.

TANYA: Jasmine.

NELLA: Nella.

TANYA: Nella?

SOPHIE: Sophie.

TANYA: And Sophie. (Derrick is at the juice table. Kali and Derrick are connecting . . . some bantering about the juice.)

DERRICK (implying that the quantity of food is sparse): Pretty light eating . . . want a sniff of the juice?

KALI: No, thanks. (Kali and Derrick are laughing.)

LUREEN: So immature. Grow up.

DERRICK: Like you, Lureen?

NELLA: She's way too mature for us. I don't know why she even comes.

TANYA (to Derrick): Do you mind sitting down so we can get started? Okay . . . so, everybody . . . I just want to talk a little bit about, um, how your week's been . . . sort of a little check-in. (Tanya is looking at Kali. Lureen is furiously filing her nails. It looks like Tanya wants to go around the circle in an orderly fashion.) Anyone want to start? (She looks at Kali. Derrick is coughing and mumbling. Sophie is looking at a magazine. Nella is sitting with her head down trying to look at the magazine.) Derrick, anything you want to say about your week? . . . Good or bad?

DERRICK: Um . . . ya . . . I think I stepped in shit, man.

NELLA: You are shit. (Sophie and Nella are talking to each other. Derrick is raising his foot toward Lureen, playfully trying to touch her with his foot.)

LUREEN (getting up): Get away from me.

TANYA (who has been focused on those three, now turns her head to the girls): Do you mind . . . putting the book away just for now so we can get started? (Sophie continues to turn pages.) Does anyone want to start? (Kali has a huge smile on his face and has a verbal exchange with Lureen, who is still filing her nails. Derrick moves around and then takes a small white ball and bounces it toward Kali. Kali responds to this with a big grin and catches the ball.) Okay . . . I'm a little concerned that we're not getting started and that we're wasting our time here.

*Feedback to Tanya from the Simulators*

DERRICK: I felt that there was very little control when we first came together. You were intentionally trying to ignore me.

JASMINE: When you called my name, I looked at you, but you didn't look at me . . . I felt you weren't paying attention to us at all. Later on, you looked at me . . .

SOPHIE: Good introduction . . . came to us . . . shook our hands . . . had good eye contact with us . . . made me feel welcome . . . I felt that you cared. When we were looking at the magazine and you wanted to take it away . . . I felt you meant business and I felt kind of afraid.

NELLA: When you asked Sophie to put the magazine away, I thought, oh, oh . . . so I took it because I felt that I still needed the cover . . . I also felt good that you shook my hand and made eye contact.

LUREEN: When you addressed me by the wrong name . . . I felt annoyed . . . but then you asked me how my week was and that made me feel important . . . When you asked Nella to sit down, I felt relieved . . . I felt that you were in control.

KALI: When you asked me how my week was, that made me feel more comfortable . . . and then when you asked to put the book down, I felt like . . . I was scared . . . I was afraid that . . . I was just afraid.

*Reflections on Tanya's Practice*

While the worker may have felt intimidated by the teens, it is obvious from the feedback that they were intimidated by her, although they had appreciated her initial welcoming overtures. It seemed that mutual fear, the antithesis of mutual aid, was a characterizing theme at the launching of this group. Without the feedback from the simulators, the student worker (and perhaps the observers) might not have understood the impact of seemingly innocuous comments by the worker to establish what she perceived as "order" in the group.

The worker's theme appeared to be "getting started." Her notion of it, however, seemed to be a preconceived idea of orderly, verbal participation of the group members with her. She didn't recognize that the group already had begun, with content being expressed in the interaction. Her verbal communication and body language displayed a flat affect, interpreted by us as her anxiety, which would be natural given the demands of the situation. Her voice held a tone of annoyance and impatience in response to her perception of the teens' lack of cooperation. Their interaction demonstrated verbal and some physical aggression (e.g., Derrick's moving behind the worker at the beginning of the meeting, his "shoe teasing" with Lureen, and his ball bouncing; Lureen's nail filing and expressed superiority; the girls' reading of the magazine), all contributing to her anxieties and interfering with her sense of "order" and control of the group. She may well have felt some fear and uncertainty about what could happen.

The worker physically turned her head away from significant things that were happening in the group. She did not participate *with* the members, appearing blind to the fact that they were creating their own group climate. Without being aware of it, she was holding herself outside of the group's beginning, impatient, ironically for it to start.

There were a number of missed opportunities for worker intervention, first with Derrick at the juice table and his remarks to Kali about the quantity of refreshments. As well, the theme of maturity raised by Nella and Lureen was ignored, even though four of the six teens were engaged in the discussion. There was no acknowledgment or response to Nella's comment about Lureen being "way too mature for us." The worker interrupted their dialogue with a request to Derrick to sit down, which he did, although the topic of maturity continued among the members. This theme could have been developed into a discussion about the commonalities they shared and the possible purposes of the group.

The worker again intervened from outside the members' group life. She lost the relevance of the live interaction of the moment by saying, "I just want to talk a little about how your week's been ... sort of a little check-in." Her turning to Kali, inviting him to speak first, implied her preference for an orderly pattern of participation.

The opportunity to respond to Derrick's comment about "stepping in shit" was missed entirely. It may have been an analogy for how his week had been. The ensuing interaction about the shoe engaged all the members but was overlooked by the worker. She also chose not to address the girls' interest in the magazine, seeing their behaviour only as a disruption to the group rather than as a means to connect with them.

By tuning into her own anxieties, even fears about the threatening air surrounding Derrick's behaviour, the worker may have been able to address, with empathy, the beginning apprehensions of the teens, thereby taking the leadership in the establishment of comfort, safety, and norms of group participation.

The teens were present in the group voluntarily; they came with some hopes and expectations but posed some challenges for the worker. Her beginning tasks needed to include: (a) helping to create safety, comfort, and acquaintance among all present, (b) enabling the teens to get to know one another in their own ways, and (c) helping to clarify the purposes of the group, that is, the ways the teens may have used the group to address their needs and issues. In the absence of this initial direction, the teens could not focus their energy or allay their anxieties.

### Excerpt #2: Student Social Worker Manuel

MANUEL: What are you looking at there, girls? Nella? (The atmosphere is relaxed and the teens are smiling. The worker maintains his focus on the girls and the magazine, while Derrick and Kali are tossing an inflated condom across the room. In response to his invitation to tell about their week, Nella complies by bounding around the outside of the circle, tapping everyone on the head, beginning a game of "Duck, Duck, Goose.") Nella, while you're going around the circle, maybe you could tell us how your week has been . . . Nella . . . OK, maybe you're not ready for this right now . . . Jasmine, how's your week been?

JASMINE: Not bad.

MANUEL: Not bad . . . anything exciting?

JASMINE: I stayed home.

MANUEL: You stayed home and didn't go to school? Derrick, did you have . . .

DERRICK: Yeah . . . I stepped in shit! Remember?

MANUEL: Oh, right . . . I'm sorry. And Nella?

NELLA: I went to school.

MANUEL: And that's it? You didn't do anything else?

NELLA: No.

(After a lull, Derrick throws a deflated condom across the floor.)

KALI: You'd better pick it up. (Another lull follows.)

MANUEL: Is that something you want to talk about in the group . . . sex?

DERRICK (in a different, more serious tone): You get off on talking about sex with young people?

NELLA: Can we have a party?

MANUEL: Sure.

DERRICK (in a singsong voice): Whatever . . .

NELLA: What are we gonna do?

MANUEL: It's your group, you guys. Come up with whatever you want to do and I'll try to help out wherever I can.

NELLA: You don't care?

MANUEL: I really do care.

NELLA: Then think of an idea.

MANUEL: I don't want to be, like, the leader of this . . . I'll just . . . sort of help out . . . where I can.

DERRICK (picking up his chair as he stands): I'll be the leader. (He sets his chair down right in front of Manuel with his back to Manuel.)

KALI (standing up, smiling): I want to be the leader.

MANUEL: So . . .

DERRICK (to Nella): Hi, Buddy.

NELLA: Hi, Derrick. (Silence.)

DERRICK (smiling, to Nella): I think I'm going to take this shoe off and beat you over the head with it.

NELLA: Oh no! I'll choke from the smell! (Silence, then group members make some quiet comments.)

MANUEL: OK . . . so this party thing . . . let's take a look at it . . . (Manuel reopens the topic of a party and checks out with the teens whether they want to pursue the planning. The response from them is unenthusiastic. They are slumped in their chairs, then become agitated.) Before we go any further with this party idea, I think we need to maybe talk about some ground rules for the group . . . 'cause a lot of people are getting pretty angry.

NELLA (shooting her hands up in the air): Yes . . . more rules!

(While this is happening, Derrick holds up a paper in front of Lureen that says "fuck off.")

LUREEN (as she tries to ignore him, takes her chair across the circle and puts it between Nella and Manuel): I just had to get away from him. (At the same time, Kali strolls across to Derrick, takes the paper in his hand, and looks at it.)

DERRICK (standing up, crossing the circle, and stopping in front of Lureen, in a low but angry tone): What do you keep looking at me for?

LUREEN (angry and frustrated): Because you're in my face. (She moves her chair back as she stands and walks toward Derrick.) I'm not scared of you!

(Derrick immediately turns and goes back to his seat.)

LUREEN (as she sits down): I'll kick your ass.

MANUEL: OK . . . um, that's the sort of thing we need to talk about.

NELLA: What's the sort of thing we should talk about?

MANUEL: The aggressiveness and violence. (Derrick and Kali are standing up together, chuckling over the "fuck off" sign.) Do we want that to happen here?

NELLA: Well, it happens everywhere else . . . (Most of the group members are responding but over one another with quiet voices; they're speaking into the centre of the group without directing it to anyone.)

LUREEN: Isn't it normal?

NELLA: Why not?

MANUEL: How come it happens everywhere else? (A tense silence follows.) Violence in the group . . . do you think it should be allowed? (As Manuel attempts to engage the teens individually in answering his question, they fidget, look elsewhere, are verbally unresponsive.) OK . . . I don't think I've really made my position clear. I work with the Children's Aid Society . . . you probably all know that . . . and you're all here for a reason . . . (Derrick starts "mooing" and someone laughs.) . . . You have dealt with physical abuse or other forms of abuse . . . (Derrick continues to "moo.") I'm trying to talk here. Could you stop . . . um . . . so my job here is as group facilitator . . . (Kali is laughing out loud and guessing "cow?" Manuel looks at the two of them and smiles.)

*Feedback to Manuel from the Simulators*

DERRICK: It was confusing for Derrick that you wouldn't really engage him . . . and so he was, like, left confused, because he's used to being engaged more than what you were offering.

JASMINE: When you went with the idea of the party, I felt that you were interested in our ideas, which made me feel really good. And then when you did not go further with it to help organize it, I was frustrated and with the distraction . . . you went from topic to topic . . .

SOPHIE: When you said you weren't the leader . . . that it was our group . . . and it was up to us to organize the party, I felt . . . OK . . . he doesn't care.

NELLA: When I first mentioned the birthday thing and you didn't pick up on it, I thought . . . "oh, nobody matters" . . . and then you went back. I thought, "OK, so maybe I do matter," and that felt good. When you asked about sex, everybody clammed up. When I said that thing about violence being everywhere, it felt really good that you got everybody to sit down and actually quiet, and took control . . . because I felt like I had triggered that.

LUREEN: You said it was up to us to decide what to do—I was scared. I felt that I needed the guidance. Later you leaned forward, like your body language was really positive, and you seemed like you cared about our lives.

KALI: I felt that you didn't care what we were doing . . . and then when you told us that you were from the Children's Aid Society and got all serious, I felt confronted and I felt taken aback—like "getting serious now"—and I was scared. But then you asked me how I was doing and I felt that you cared and that you were actually focusing on me and what we were doing.

*Reflections on Manuel's Practice*

Issues of leadership as an aspect of the worker's role were evident in Manuel's practice. The group still very much needed the worker to perform a leadership function in the clear establishment of the purposes of this group and in bringing the members together to become acquainted with one another. Until members have some information about the others and their mutual commonalities, and about what the group will be like, they have little basis for a beginning sense of connection and belonging. The work of beginning this group has barely begun. The uncertainty of Manuel's approach to leadership (e.g., Manuel's assertion that he was not the leader . . . "It's your group!") and then his display of authority ("I work with the Children's Aid Society") was confusing for the group members and contributed to their continuing anxieties and their inability to define the group's purposes.

When Manuel intervened by asking the group members if there was anything they wanted to talk about, he gave no parameters about what would be possible and acceptable topics to raise in the group. As a result, suggesting anything was too risky for the teens. Elaboration of members' input to draw others into the activity did not happen. He did not use opportunities to illuminate commonalities shared by members. It was an individualizing exercise and was followed by a long period of fidgeting and anxiousness.

When members made personal statements (e.g., Nella's comment about violence), the worker missed the opportunity to focus on them so that other group members could express the topics' relevance for them. During a "time-out," a classmate suggested to Manuel that "when the discussion's around violence . . . I think that's a really important discussion to have, and that was a great way that you brought it up. I also think that with these kids in particular, you need to get them to define violence . . . to understand where they're coming from." Although the discussion at that moment involved input from everyone, the worker was not able to make the links among the members and their respective remarks. He seemed to lose his connection with them and the very important content being expressed individually by them. They were expressing a commonly shared familiarity with violence, but the worker bypassed the opportunity to engage with them on what they meant by violence, and what violence means to them, when he asked, "Should violence be allowed in the group?" It is understandable and essential for the worker to establish a norm of nonviolence in the group, but, at this moment, in attempting to generate "intellectual discussion" about allowing violence in the group, some affective realities of the group life also were ignored. The exchange between Derrick and Lureen was intensely charged with threat and danger. The worker's attention to both their behaviour and the feelings of all present may have moved the group toward some clarity about its purposes and potential as a safe context for dealing with difficult issues. He was acting on earlier input from the instructor but missed the current relevance for the members. Workers' inclination to refocus, conceptualize, and interpret content prematurely may keep them out of the immediacy of the moment, causing them to lose a precious entry point for joining with the members on significant material.

During the interaction, when Derrick threw a deflated condom across the floor, Manuel raised the question of whether the group members would like to talk about sex in the group. Derrick's response, "You get off talking about sex with young people?" effectively stopped Manuel's intervention. Manuel appeared to have made the topic unspeakable, even though it might have been appropriate. Sex is an issue of content that was visible in the group, but in the absence of discussion about group purpose, the members didn't know what could be a legitimate and safe topic. Without parameters and contracting, the members did not know why they were there.

### Excerpt #3: Student Social Worker Amy

DERRICK (to Jasmine): Are you afraid your dad's gonna beat you?

JASMINE: Maybe.

DERRICK: You should kill him . . . I know a couple of guys you could pay.

NELLA (following some verbal exchange with Derrick): I wish you could kill my mom's boyfriend.

AMY: Why would you want to kill your mom's boyfriend?

NELLA: Mm . . . 'cause he's my mom's boyfriend.

AMY: A bit of a creep?

NELLA: Well . . . nooo . . . well, I don't know . . . they're always together. I don't really know my mom. My dad . . . I don't even know where my dad is.

LUREEN: You're better off that way.

NELLA: Why?

LUREEN: Cause why *would* you want to know your dad?

NELLA: Well, it's better than some stinky old farty boyfriend.

LUREEN: Yeah, well, if you got to know your dad, you'd probably be disappointed anyway.

NELLA: Yeah, but he'd be real. (The worker, all this time, makes no comments, nor does she intervene during this discussion. She's trying to listen to the girls, but she's being distracted by Derrick and Kali, who are joking together noisily. Amy calls "time-out.")

(Amy tries to incorporate class and instructor feedback of naming and summarizing the themes. As soon as she says, "Dads aren't great," Derrick immediately groans, gets up, walks across the room, asks Kali if he farted, and they start joking around.)

AMY: I'm thinking this is something we can talk about later . . . maybe in a later session . . .

NELLA: Why later?

AMY: I don't know . . . we can talk about it now . . . Derrick and Kali don't seem interested in it.

NELLA: They don't have to talk about it . . . they aren't doing anything bad . . . they're just being there.

AMY: They're just being idiots, eh? Do you agree with that? (looking at Derrick) Do you agree with that, that you guys are being idiots?

DERRICK: She just narked you out, man.

NELLA: *I* didn't say you're being idiots.

DERRICK (to Nella, and pointing to Amy): Not you! *She* did it.

(Amy then moves on by raising the issue of planning a party the next week for Nella's birthday. The group members become involved in this with some energy; different members offer to bring food items. The group session ends focusing on the party.)

*Feedback to Amy from the Simulators*

DERRICK: It wasn't going anywhere. This was really confusing to him, like you weren't engaging him in any way.

JASMINE: When you brought back the idea of having a party and helping to organize it, I felt . . . we're going to do something. When you wrapped up, you went very quickly, so I thought, I don't want to leave yet . . . but I looked forward to next week because you wrapped up with an idea—a plan.

SOPHIE: I liked the way you had a soothing voice. It made me feel comfortable. I felt . . . we were going to get somewhere. I liked how you checked in with all of us at the end. I felt . . . next week we have a plan, and we're going to get something done.

NELLA: When I started talking about my mom's boyfriend, you picked up on that and made me feel really good because it's like somebody does care about this. How you got the four of us involved in talking about the men in our lives, that was important to me. When you got involved in the party, that felt really good because it was my birthday.

LUREEN: When you sat down, you leaned forward, and I felt relaxed. But then when you started talking about the birthday party, I began to feel excluded because I had already told you I wasn't coming.

KALI: When you focused on the four girls and you didn't focus on Derrick or I, I felt unwanted. You didn't care that I was there . . . Then, when you asked us if we felt we were acting like idiots, I felt even more stupid . . . and I felt *really* belittled when you asked me if I was feeling like an idiot. But then, right at the end, you reaffirmed what we were doing next week, and I said that I was bringing ice cream. I was part of the group.

*Reflection on Amy's Practice*

Despite the efforts of the worker to engage in a natural social manner with the teens, she listened to content issues of great importance to them without acknowledging or attempting to develop them. Interestingly, while some of the observers perceived Amy's nonverbal behaviour to be rude and unengaging (e.g., eating cookies throughout the discussion, responding to comments in a "rote" manner, using a fairly monotone voice), feedback from the simulators indicated that for some of them, her voice and manner were "soothing."

Relationships with parents clearly were meaningful to the members, and specific thoughts and feelings were shared. The worker's responses to Nella's and Lureen's poignant discussion about dads and men did little to further the discussion or engage the rest of the group members in a difficult but important topic. This may also be related to the fact that even by the end of the session, group purposes still were not defined. As the instructor suggested during a "time-out," it could be useful to "go through some of the themes and then try and bring it together," but in their own words. Instead of staying with the girls and their discussion, the attention of the worker went to the boys, whom she deemed to be uninterested in the topic. It is significant in terms of the building of connectedness among the members that, in reaction to the worker's criticism of the boys ("They're just being idiots, eh?"), they were able to voice their solidarity against her ("*I* didn't say you're being idiots." . . . "Not you! *She* did it.").

The simulators' feedback to Amy was mixed. They regarded positively the "action" taken around the party plans, perhaps because, by this time in the life of the group, the members were desperate for some common focus. They expressed experiencing a sense of caring from the worker, though it may have been preferable for them to feel valued in their tentative, but very important, excursions into their serious content concerns. The negative responses, particularly from Kali and Derrick, reflected how the worker's casual remarks about them being "idiots," which she may have believed were "cool," were, in fact, insensitive and hurtful. The simulators' reflections demonstrate how feedback directly related to experiential learning can focus on differential impacts of workers' behaviours.

## FINAL REFLECTIONS ON GROUP SIMULATION

The use of simulated clients in the classroom presents a learning opportunity for instructors as well. When used at the beginning of a course, it can identify areas of existing knowledge and skill in the student pool and, therefore, aspects of the course content which will need particular emphasis. How we proceed to teach a class may be influenced by what is observed in a group simulation early in the term. The luxury of a second simulation toward the end of the course could be useful to consolidate the learning, to show students what skill areas still may need to be developed, and to feature the skills they have learned well.

As an experiential learning opportunity that most resembles a real practice situation, but with the safety of being artificial, a group simulation assists students in understanding the value of the groupworker being *real* as a person. We need to teach students to cross the barrier between person and professional in order that their interventive role, and the nature of group process facilitated, are experienced as authentic and relevant by the members. Students, as the worker with a group, often latch onto concrete tasks, as in our class simulation each worker encouraged the teens to plan a birthday party. In preparing a class, and in giving instructional input during and after a simulation, it is important to direct the student workers' focus on the live, multidimensional, interactional dynamics among the members, as well as on the cognitive processing of content and tasks.

NANCY: Someone previously used the term "testing" . . . [The group members] want to know what you're about and what they can expect from you . . . You know how we talked about how content issues may not be said explicitly . . . Sometimes people act out those issues or contribute to them indirectly, so in the here-and-now life of *this* group, Derrick was bringing a piece of content [threatening to hit Nella with his shoe] . . . that would be something the worker could latch on to right now: "What did I hear you say? What's that about? Is that the kind of group we want here? Do we want that kind of thing happening in *our* group?"

For example, instructor feedback to Manuel, as he was struggling, suggested that the group members wanted to know what they could expect from him, that content issues might not be said explicitly, and that sometimes people cut out those issues in the here-and-now life of the group. Group process has three elements: content, affect, and the social interaction that serves as the vehicle for the work of the group. All need active monitoring and intervention in a natural, social manner, grounded in a solid base of knowledge for practice.

The simulation was an intense classroom experience for everyone. It felt authentic, and it engaged the focus and energy of us all in the struggle to work with this challenging group. The powerful experiential learning occurred in four dimensions: personally for the students, whether they were playing the worker or observing; from the feedback given by each simulated group member; from the teaching points offered by the two instructors present; and, significantly, from the constructive and supportive input shared by student peers in the class. Their excellent observational skills, sensitivity in articulating praise, and helpful critiquing were remarkably evident. The experience served as a rallying point for the class, expediting the development of a collegial mutual support and aid learning environment. Though a class is not a group, a collective approach to the learning process may usefully and enjoyably assist in the integration of course content for groupworkers in the making, firmly establishing their foundation of knowledge for social work practice with groups.

## APPENDIX: GROUP MEMBER PROFILES

At thirteen, Nella is the youngest member. She is in grade seven and has done well at school, though not consistently. She is an only child and is of English descent, with roots in Maritime Canada. She has never known her biological father, having lived most of her childhood with her mother and serial stepfathers. N is in foster care, with Crown Wardship pending, and she sees her mother frequently on weekends. Her mother has an alcohol problem, has had multiple marital partners, and appears not to play a strong parental role with N. After their visits, N often is distraught, expressing frustration and confusion at her mother's demands and behaviour. N is quick to laugh and cry in the group, socially outgoing, but reticent when troubled by a painful issue. She relates with the boys in the group often through physical behaviour—slapping, punching, kicking—and speaks of regular episodes of street fighting with peers. N, as well, is fun loving and very much interested in boys.

Sophie is thirteen, almost fourteen, and is in an alternate public school program which allows her to attend evening classes at a grade seven to eight level. She seems to have many free hours each day, which she spends with other young people. Alcohol, sex, drugs, and theft are mentioned by S as part of their activities. S has been living with her parents and sisters, all of whom immigrated into Canada from Portugal several years ago. S rejects the cultural restrictions which her parents attempt to impose on her. This creates friction in the family, to which her father responds with physical violence. S enters a foster home during the course of the group due to a physical attack on her by her father. Her mother appears supportive of her daughter but, like S, is under the authority of her husband. S is quiet in the group, rarely speaking on her own behalf, although a number of times she urges N to speak. She and N are previously acquainted with each other from their neighbourhood.

Kali is fourteen, of Indo-Caribbean ancestry, with bright academic potential. He attends grade seven at a public school, although his grades seem to be suffering at this time. Upon arriving in Canada, he and his family spent some years in Montreal, where he learned to speak French. He is living with his mother and stepfather but does not get along with the latter. There seems to be a mutually desired relationship between him and his mother which can be demonstrated only when the stepfather is not present. K, otherwise, appears to be treated as if unwanted in the home. K is sociable in the group, alert to interpersonal dynamics and the unspoken feelings of members. He serves the group as an activator, a peacemaker, and an entertainer to relieve tension. K, too, has experienced severe physical abuse by parent figures, although, in contrast to D, he consciously attempts to restrain himself from instigating violence with others. K has an engaging charm, which, in combination with his astuteness about people, makes him a positive presence in the group.

Jasmine is fourteen and in grade ten at a Catholic school. She is a serious girl who laughs little in the group. She expresses curiosity about the social relating of the other members with one another but does not engage in it easily with them. English is J's second language, and it seems that her comprehension is better than her ability to express herself. Her family arrived here from South America about two years ago, and J speaks with some sadness of aspects of life left behind in the move, for example, going to the beach. J lives with her mother, father, and several brothers, older and younger than she. The father, as the senior male, appears to exert a great deal of authority over all family members and enforces his control through the use of physical violence. J has been in a foster home on at least one occasion as the result of physical abuse by her father.

Lureen, at fifteen, is the oldest group member. She is in grade eleven and does well academically at a Catholic school. As a child, she lived with her parents and a younger sister. The family came to Canada from Portugal when L was small, and, although she speaks with pride of her national heritage, she has grown up mostly in Canada and speaks English with no Portuguese accent. L has been in foster care for some time, and is a Crown Ward, having experienced severe physical and emotional abuse from her parents and other relatives. L presents herself as "cool" and mature, saying that she has risen above all the problems caused her by her family. She expects little from them now and, in fact, has minimal contact with them. In the group, L appears often to be bored with the behaviours of the other members and disdainful of their "immaturity."

Derrick is fourteen, of South American Spanish background, and in grade nine at a public school. He lives with his younger sister and his mother, who has had numerous marital partners. His family is fragmented and fluid in arrangement: immediate and extended members frequently move and regroup. D has been passed between his mother and father, experiencing short-lived periods of settledness, and has experienced physical abuse by his parents. D presents himself as pseudomature, at times displaying authoritarian behaviours, which he attempts to enforce through the use of threats of physical violence. He speaks of having gotten good grades as a young child, but now he is failing and chronically truant. D typically appears as a powder keg. He is angry and sullen, expressing himself with an air of hopelessness. A lighter, playful, humorous side of D is sometimes visible, but a heavy overlay is more often present. D imposes a strong influence in the group, as he commands attention either verbally or through various noises and mannerisms, and he uses his physical strength to intimidate the other members. D is hospitalized for psychiatric care toward the end of the group, for circumstances which never become clear except that they involve his mother, violence, and some threat of suicide on D's part. D's behaviour in the group is unpredictable and volatile. He darts from distracting playfully from what others are doing by making animal noises to speaking tearfully of his feelings of being alone and unloved to lunging suddenly across the room to grab someone who has offended him.

# REFERENCES

Barsky, A., Rogers, G., Krysik, J., and Langevin, P. (1997). Building a community of learners: Innovations in course design. Paper presented at the CASSW/ ACESS Conference and Learned Societies, St. John's, Newfoundland.

Kenyon, G. (1995). Live simulation in field instructor training. In Rogers, G. (Ed.), *Social work field education: Views and visions* (pp. 174-184). Dubuque, IA: Kendall/Hunt.

Kurland, R. and Salmon, R. (1998). *Teaching a methods course in social work with groups.* Alexandria, VA: CSWE.

Papell, C. (1997). Dilemmas in social work education in these challenging times. In Sachdev, P., Burford, G., Cregheur, L., Kimberley, D., and Hurley, A. (Eds.), *Trends in social work education* (pp. 5-23). School of Social Work, Memorial University of Newfoundland.

Chapter 10

# Creating Loss Support Groups for the Elderly

Beverly S. Ryan
Patty Crawford

In any senior housing community there are multiple layers of loss: loss of health, loss of mobility, loss of vision, hearing, and cognitive abilities. All the residents have moved away from their primary residences, perhaps the homes in which they raised their families. Their role in society has shifted after retirement. As Betty Friedan stated, "For vital age, a project that structures one's day and keeps alive those all-important human ties and sense of personhood is essential" (1993, p. 225). This is a new stage of life. The residents have weathered change before, but this time their support system is narrowed by the loss of those in their cohort. Many of these losses are experienced over a shorter period of time. "All I do is go to funerals" is a frequently heard comment. Their friends who shared in their lives are caught in the same whirlpool of change.

They have found a new home in a senior complex, housing designed to provide privacy and safety. The facility's advertising promotes the service-rich environment that will provide for all their needs: meals, housekeeping, health care, activities, church services, transportation, cable TV, and emergency pull-cords. The family works to create an environment that resembles "home." However, the front door opens into a hallway and not onto the street and into the neighborhood. Regrettably, after the monumental task of moving a parent, many adult children must return to their own work and family obligations, perhaps in distant locations. The resident faces the challenge of discovering the new community alone.

Their resident handbook is their guide to this new world. It states that mealtime is at 5:00 p.m., the post office truck will arrive at 2:15 p.m. every Wednesday, and the grocery van will be at the entrance at 9:15 a.m. every Tuesday. The book warns that they cannot keep their doors open because of the heating and cooling systems in the buildings and that the fire code requires a door closer and that residents will be instructed if there is a need to evacuate during an emergency. The pages of information are detailed. The residents' adjustment is complicated by the technical language they confront in their own health care and its delivery systems, and insurance can befuddle the otherwise wise.

This stage of life requires many skills to navigate. As Mary Pipher states in her book, *Another Country,* "It requires courage, forbearance, stoicism, and the abilities to laugh and forget problems. And it requires the ability to assert needs, to communicate openly, and to process pain. Successful resolution of this stage allows the old to feel respected and at peace with their families" (1999, p. 127). Unfortunately, many people at this point in life are experiencing bereavement overload and do not have these skills available.

Withdrawal and isolation can result if connections are not made with other residents and staff. As Joan Barry (1988) wrote, "These questions are even more salient for the elderly people who lose roles (such as worker or spouse) and are marginalized by society. As Zastrow wrote 'the identity we develop is largely dependent upon our involvement with others.' So, if they are isolated from others, many people become unsure of who they are" (p. 451). Statistics show that geriatric depression "rises dramatically in institutional settings in the presence of co-morbid medical illnesses, mounting disability and physical deterioration" (Leszcz, 1997, p. 90).

Society has tried to address the challenges of aging often by external means. We have developed enlightened architecture and care delivery systems. We pounce upon new color schemes for their psychological effect. We join together in hotel banquet rooms to discuss regulations and management of senior facilities. Seldom do we recognize that we are building our own future. We rarely look toward the inner strengths that our elders possess and the resource they can provide. We act as if a group of aliens has landed in our midst, and we don't know how to host their arrival. We miss opportunities to create community that can support, heal, and build new relationships. "Elders are not as vulnerable as portrayed in ageist stereotypes; they can deal with painful issues when provided with the opportunity, and they can benefit from the experience in terms of enhanced relationships and improved self-esteem" (Wood and Seymour, 1994, p. 19).

It is our goal in this chapter to present loss support groups as one vehicle to tap the inner strength of our elders and create community through group work. For participants, these groups can provide normalization of their grief, recognition of the depth of their loss, the value of openness, and a support system that reaches beyond their family and their health care providers. These support groups can unleash the strength of community, something that those born in the early part of the twentieth century understand from their youth. We reach for their wisdom.

The senior apartment community we speak of is divided into four individual buildings with public congregating areas on the main level. It houses 420 residents. The residents range in age from 65 to 104 years. The majority of the residents are Caucasian from a midwestern background. Home Health Care is available on the premises, on a fee-for-service basis. While the community tends to be outwardly social in the public areas, many find themselves outside a social group. People meet in the dining room during congregate meals and enjoy entertainment, but most entertainment is of a passive type and geared toward reaching a large number of people: movies, performances, games, and lectures. While appreciated, these organized activities do not provide the opportunity to interact in smaller groups or to discuss the deeper things that affect life.

## SEEING THE NEED

As staff members, we observed an initial outpouring of support for the griever at the time of a death. There were sympathy cards, flowers, visits from clergy, and funeral attendance. But as the weeks passed, residents reported feeling that friends were avoiding them. When questioned further, residents admitted their perception that friends were uncomfortable and reluctant to make conversation. "They don't know what to say. It's just easier for them to avoid me" (personal communication, 1997).

As we visited with residents in their apartments, we discovered a prevailing sense of loneliness in those who had lost close family and friends to death. These residents tended to isolate more and avoid large group activities. Somatic symptoms began to appear. The home care staff, the social worker, and the resident service coordinator began to identify residents whose appearances were changing, who were losing weight, and who were only coming out of their apartments to retrieve the mail. Also, families would telephone, asking, "How can we get Mom more involved? She is just sitting in her apartment. What can we do?" Physicians, receptionists, and other residents also expressed concerns. A formal needs assessment seemed a poor use of time. It was time to take action. The Loss Support Groups in the geographic area, usually at hospitals or churches, would require transportation away from the facility. Many residents were also reluctant to go out at night.

We, the resident service coordinator and the home care social worker, submitted a proposal to pilot a grief and loss support group. This proposal outlined our purpose, number of sessions, setting and time, and sample topics. We presented it to the director of housing and the Home Care administrator. With their blessing, the first Grief and Loss Support Group was announced to the community through the internal monthly newsletter. In her column, the director of housing invited readers to contact the resident service coordinator if they were interested in taking part in the support group. The newsletter announcement brought no response. In some ways, this was not surprising. The concept of support groups was unfamiliar to the majority of the community. Lund, Dimond, and Juretich have explored the characteristics of potential participants in grief support groups. They discovered that most of those who were willing to participate in self-help groups historically had had a large and helpful support network. They also noted that "elderly people might be reluctant to participate because they perceive the intervention as a psychological treatment and wish to avoid the associated stigma" (198, p. 312).

We reviewed our list of bereaved residents who had been referred to us and decided to talk to them individually. The resident service coordinator delivered face-to-face invitations, explaining when and where the group would be held, what could happen in the group, and that the group would include others who had experienced similar loss. This personal contact proved to be helpful in several ways.

The one-to-one visit started the review of their grief and intro-duced the idea of processing the experience. Pictures and other mem-orabilia brought forth reminiscence. The chance to talk about their grief was something they longed for. "My son doesn't want me to dwell on it [the death of her husband]" (personal communication, 1998).

The visit validated their loss and acknowledged the difficult time they were going through. The visit offered them an opportunity to learn about the grief process. When they viewed the support group as education, they were more willing to participate.

The one-to-one visit helped to shape workable groups. Some with more recent loss wanted to be kept in mind for the following group, feeling it was too painful to share at this time. The visit established a positive rapport with one of the facilitators, who could also be a con-tact person for follow-up questions.

For the purpose of this chapter, we have melded the observations from different groups to provide an overview of our experiences. As facilitators, following each session, we debriefed and compiled a de-tailed journal of each evening's observations. What began as an obli-gation to management turned out to be a valuable learning tool for us as facilitators. The observations made during these debriefing ses-sions led us to better understand the group dynamics and the benefits of the dual-facilitator structure.

## PLANNING THE SESSIONS

We decided to create a closed group because the subject matter was very personal and it was important to build continuity and trust among the participants. A quiet party room away from the main traf-fic areas was chosen. The comfortable sofas and chairs created a home-like atmosphere. It was private and located within the complex. We chose to hold the group in the early evening, as there were many activities scheduled during the day. However, after the dinner hour there were few events. Sessions were scheduled to begin at 6:30 p.m. and end at 8:00 p.m. A helpful phone reminder would be provided the morning of each session. We planned six sessions to run over a twelve-week period. This format could allow each resident time to process information shared and to advance in his or her personal journey through grief.

In the one-to-one visits, we heard a clear message of the residents' desire to learn more about grief. We created session plans with topics to provide structure, then scheduled in open discussion time. Each group session included a short review of the previous session, a topic for the evening, and discussion. The last thirty minutes were devoted to refreshments and socialization.

At the first group, each participant was given a packet containing an outline and a set of guidelines printed in large type. We reviewed the information as a group. To most participants, group work was new and unexplored territory, and they needed encouragement to move beyond superficial social interactions. The guidelines encouraged everyone to share in the conversation and also gave permission to "pass" on questions they felt they were not emotionally ready to respond to. We talked about the cathartic effect of tears. This population was unaccustomed to outward displays of emotion. They wanted to stop tears and to quiet feelings. Also, group members came from a generation of people who thought that giving advice was truly helping another person. As facilitators, we gave them permission not to "fix" a problem and were watchful for such situations. Confidentiality was a concern because all the participants lived in the same complex. Few would be willing to share if they knew their personal pain would be discussed over dinner with other residents in the facility. We asked them to refrain from using names or specific details about the group but encouraged them to discuss their own feelings with family and friends.

### Session One: Introduction

The first session was designed to review the outline and the guidelines, and to share personal history. We arrived and placed the comfortable residential furniture in a circle. We encouraged the participants to share their stories of loss. The details of their losses emerged, each with a date and time as if the event had just happened. "The nursing home called me at 3:20 a.m. Abner was not doing well. I sat on the edge of my bed and talked to the nurse on the phone. They suggested I come to his room. I made that long walk by myself" (personal communication, 1998).

We ended the evening on a positive, social note, with an uplifting reading followed by coffee and a homemade snack. We did this out of concern for those returning home alone. The participant response was rewarding. It also inspired members of the group to share their culinary talents. When we left, we often had a volunteer to provide the treat for the following week.

### Session Two: Physical Aspects of Grief

For the fragile senior, prolonged loss of sleep, poor appetite, and change in concentration can result in failure to thrive. This could precipitate a further loss of independence. It is not unusual to see an illness or injury following a loss. Many participants did not recognize the connection between the physical symptoms they were experiencing and their personal loss. This session was also an opportunity to discuss tears. Many expressed a struggle to keep them back, feeling that they were a sign of weakness or an inability to cope. "When the choir sang on Sunday, I had to leave. The music reminded me of Nils. I went to the bathroom and cried" (personal communication, 1998).

The death of a spouse or significant friend interrupts the routines of daily life. Residents reported that resocializing as a single person became a challenge. It was difficult to go to the dining room alone. It was also a challenge to assume new roles and responsibilities. Some had never written a check or were unaware of their spouse's investment strategies. Cooking and grocery shopping were mysteries to some. Attendance at family gatherings was painful without their partners. Some mentioned that family members were reluctant to talk about the loss, fearful that they would bring on "emotions."

### Session Three: The Emotions

In this session we reviewed other, perhaps less obvious, emotions connected to the grief process. We found it interesting that there was a resistance to the inclusion of anger as a normal response to loss. Most of the group members did not feel justified in being angry. Some could view other people's anger as OK because of unusual circumstances such as accidents or foul play. Connections between the feelings of abandonment and anger were also difficult for them to acknowledge. Ironically, many expressed the wish to have "gone first."

A few participants identified relief as an emotion that they felt. It was usually in connection with a release from illness, pain, and the confines of an institution. One group member felt guilty because the death was so unexpected, even though her husband had been 98 and in a nursing home. The most prevalent emotion identified was that of loneliness. The feeling of loneliness far outranked the feeling of fear. We theorize that perhaps what they had experienced was their greatest fear.

### Session Four: Does a Relationship Exist with the Deceased?

In this session we explored what happens to relationships after death. We invited participants to bring photos of their loved ones. Some brought shopping bags full. Their selections were fascinating. Some chose pictures from their courtship, others the most recent or last photo. One brought an obituary and photo from a newspaper article about her brother's mules. The photo was of the mules, and the obituary was told from the mules' point of view. The participants agreed that it was common for those grieving to have conversations and feel the presence of their loved ones. There were visible signs of comfort in the group when they found that others felt the same way. They smiled and reached out to one another. Their unanimous opinion was that a relationship does continue after death. As Worden (1991) has stated, "The task is . . . not to help the bereaved give up their relationship with the deceased, but to help them find an appropriate place for the dead in their emotional lives—a place that will enable them to go on living effectively in the world" (p. 17).

### Session Five: What Causes Pain and What Brings Comfort?

We discussed in this session pain and comfort. Some participants who were further along in the grieving process felt that photos and memories brought comfort. Those newer to loss sometimes avoided reminiscence because it caused pain. The group at this stage required little, if any, facilitation. A cohesive group had formed. Participants were leaving together, walking each other home, and suggesting they share a meal. Phone numbers were exchanged. This is in keeping with the findings of Caserta and Lund (1996): "The members who had contact perceived the interaction to be valuable because, as they reported, they became close to their fellow participants and wanted to preserve and extend the opportunity they had in the group meetings to express themselves to others who had experienced a loss" (p. 551). An "installation of hope" in their attitude became evident (Yalom, 1975, p. 6).

## Session Six: Review, Reflection, Closing Ritual

Our last session was a review of our experience in the group. The participants assessed their feelings. Throughout this session it was not unusual to talk about the first loss experience, usually that of a parent. Also, the discussion went further back into the histories of their relationships with their loved ones, often discussing courtships and significant life events. This was in sharp contrast to the first session, when the stories centered on the moment of death.

During the final session, we assisted in the completion of a simple, large-print evaluation form. We invited comments and criticisms that would help in the formation of future groups. We read the evaluation aloud. This provided an opportunity to review the topics and discussions that had taken place at each session. Responses were rated as very helpful, somewhat helpful, and not helpful. Pencils were provided and help was offered to those who requested it. We recognized that the results could be skewed by our presence. We wanted everyone to have the opportunity to respond and review. (Poor vision, arthritic hands, and forgetfulness are all barriers to completing a take-home evaluation.) We also offered the opportunity to contact a facilitator at a later time if they felt there were issues they preferred not to discuss within the group.

A candle-lighting ceremony concluded the session. Each person lit a candle and spoke about those they had loved and lost. It was heartfelt. Each shed tears for the others. Paul Alexander's song "Light a Candle" completed the ceremony. All the participants expressed a sense of closure. It also provided closure for us as a group.

## GROUP RESPONSE AND EVALUATION

The overall group response was positive. The later sessions ranked higher in satisfaction, possibly because of the increasing trust level and group cohesiveness. Participants favored holding the group every other week because it made the commitment feel less overwhelming. The time of day was convenient. They liked the phone call reminders we provided before each session. One of the key elements gleaned from the evaluation was the necessity for a personal invitation. Group members agreed they would not have been motivated to attend if they had only seen a notice in the elevator or in the newsletter. Ending with a social time and lighter conversation was appreciated.

### Unexpected Discoveries

We began our first group arranged in a circle, seated on sofas and soft chairs. We later found that participants were more comfortable around the oval table in the room. The straight-backed armchairs were easier to get in and out of, their walkers and canes were out of sight, and they could hear and see more clearly. They took notes, touched hands, and were more involved in the improved arrangement.

Groups of twelve functioned well, but when we observed the following group with eight participants, they seemed to share more openly. Hearing was also less difficult in a smaller group.

Initially, the closing routine of coffee and treats seemed a polite necessity to this community. Further examination revealed its therapeutic worth: it helped to build new friendships, it provided transition, and it offered an opportunity to share culinary talents. These homemade treats were a tangible gift and a chance to express appreciation to each other.

The sharing of the photographs put a real face on the loss. It created empathy and was a major factor in the development of group cohesiveness. Another, less anticipated step in creating group cohesiveness was the discussion of a relationship continuing after death. It became evident that few had shared with others the fact that they still talked to their loved one or felt his or her presence. This brought to our minds Yalom's (1975, p. 3) curative factors of universality and imparting of information.

### Positive Outcomes

Making the grief process a shared experience opens a door in the life of the older citizen. Group members were observed approaching others who had experienced a recent loss. In their small numbers, they were empowered to speak of grief openly. They carried their sharing into their families. A son reported, "Mom talks about Dad when we get together. We're not afraid to bring Dad's name into conversation!" (personal communication, 1999). Another woman delivered a box of mementos from her deceased husband so that on Christmas Eve the grandchildren could choose something that had emotional significance to them. A woman, who at first would hide her tears, wept openly with the group at the candle-lighting ceremony. Some group participants who experienced another significant loss reviewed materials they had received in the group. Participants told of sharing the inspirational readings with family, friends, and church groups.

### *Opportunities for Further Exploration*

It would be interesting to measure the effect on health and wellness that grief intervention provides. How does participation in a grief and loss support group affect the dying process of individual members? Does resolution of bereavement have an effect on the processing of grief in a participant's extended family? Can loss strengthen the bonds of family? These are some of the reasons to go on with new studies.

### *Challenges*

The major challenges in creating grief and loss support groups in senior facilities include the shortage of available personnel, funding, and time. Creating groups and inviting the participants takes time. A visit to explain the concept of a loss support group and discuss their personal loss takes an hour or more. But the bottom line isn't money. As Mary Pipher eloquently states in *Another Country,* "For accountable businessmen . . . the bottom line isn't money. It is knowing people well enough to be truly useful" (1999, p. 88). Creating opportunities for our elders to use their inner strengths and wisdom builds a climate of respect for all ages. It is our future. It is our hope.

### REFERENCES

Alexander, P. (1993). Light a candle [recorded by artist]. On *Paul Alexander: Light a Candle* [cassette recording]. Diamond Bar, CA: Jimmy Mac Studios.

Barry, J. (1988) Autobiographical writing: an effective tool for practice with the oldest old. *Social Work 33*(5):449-451.

Caserta, M.S. and Lund, D.A. (1996). Beyond bereavement support group meetings: Exploring outside social contacts among the members. *Death Studies 20*(6):537-556.

Friedan, B. (1993). *The fountain of age.* New York: Simon and Schuster.

Leszcz, M. (1997). Integrated group psychotherapy for the treatment of depression in the elderly. *Group 21*(2):89-113.

Lund, D.A., Dimond, M., and Juretich, M. (1985). Bereavement support groups for the elderly: Characteristics of potential participants. *Death Studies 9*(3-4):309-321.

Pipher, M. (1999). *Another country.* New York: Riverhead Books.

Wood, A. and Seymour, L.M. (1994). Psychodynamic group therapy for older adults: The life experiences group. *Journal of Psychosocial Nursing and Mental Health Services 32*(7):19-24.

Worden, W. (1991). *Grief counseling and grief therapy: A handbook for the mental health practitioner* (Second edition). New York: Springer.

Yalom, I.D. (1975). *The theory and practice of group psychotherapy.* New York: Basic Books.

Chapter 11

# Making Curriculum Purposeful in Group Work with Persons with Severe Mental Illnesses

Marshall Rubin

A growing trend toward curriculum-driven groups is cause for concern. The prevalence of such groups seems to be increasing. These are not groups that have a suggested curriculum. Rather, they are truly curriculum-*driven* with preset content that is to be applied without flexibility and according to a predetermined timetable. They are called groups, but they certainly are not social work groups. Perhaps they might be called classes, but actually they are not good classes either. (Kurland and Malekoff, 1998)

Papell and Rothman (1980) recognized the need for group workers to sensitively utilize what they referred to as the "mainstream model" of social work knowledge and skills to address the growing tendency to rely on rigidly structured curriculum. They wrote:

For the social group worker with a clear mainstream model identification, the mechanical use of such programmed resources, now available from clearinghouses and developers, is unlikely; but it is necessary for the social work practitioner to re-examine and reaffirm social work's basic professional model so that such convenient resources will be used in the context of the profession's purposes, knowledge, and skills. . . . The utility of the structured approach can best be realized when the social group worker places it within the flexible framework of the mainstream model. (p. 20)

## CURRICULUM-DRIVEN PRACTICE AND THE SOCIAL GROUP WORK VACUUM IN PSYCHOSOCIAL REHABILITATION AGENCIES

Mainstream model mutual aid principles, skills, and processes can be utilized to minimize pressures that lead to curriculum-driven practice in these agencies, which are commonly referred to as psychosocial rehabilitation agencies or programs. Currently, there are close to 500 agencies or programs that are organizational members of the International Association of Psychosocial Rehabilitation Services (IAPSRS), which was incorporated in 1974. There are, additionally, 1,500–2,000 agencies that offer psychosocial rehabilitation services but are not organizational members of IAPSRS. Many of the 1,400 people who have joined IAPSRS as individual members work in these nonaffiliated agencies. Most psychosocial rehabilitation programs are in the United States; the second largest number is in Canada. Psychosocial rehabilitation programs today occur in a variety of community-based settings. Many of these include clubhouses, lodges, and other stand-alone rehabilitation facilities. Others are offered as components of comprehensive community mental health agencies. Psychosocial rehabilitation services are also offered as rehabilitation components of some state hospitals and other inpatient facilities. In all of these settings, work with groups makes up a significant portion of the services.

In the 1960s, which were the early days of psychosocial rehabilitation, social group work was a core practice that was very evident when one visited the thirteen founding agencies whose executive directors met together annually to share program innovations prior to the formal establishment of IAPSRS. Many of the founding directors were trained as social group workers. The others employed social group workers in key program leadership roles. The mutual aid philosophy of social group work offered a skill base to address the normalizing, nonmedical model programs that psychosocial rehabilitation agencies seek to implement. Unfortunately, at the same time that deinstitutionalization of the 1970s and 1980s brought about a great growth in psychosocial rehabilitation services, many schools of social work stopped teaching group work. Therefore, a pool of trained social group workers was not available to meet the burgeoning staffing needs of the new psychosocial rehabilitation agencies. IAPSRS defines psychosocial rehabilitation as:

> Psychosocial rehabilitation programs for persons with mental illness provide experiences which improve ability to function in the community. The philosophy emphasizes common sense, practical needs and usually includes vocational and personal adjustment services geared toward the prevention of unnecessary hospitalization. The psychosocial rehabilitation setting is purposefully informal to reduce the psychological distance between staff and members as active participants in program planning. Members are continually encouraged to assume productive citizen roles both within the psychosocial rehabilitation facilities and in the broader community which is viewed as an integral part of the total psychosocial rehabilitation setting. (1985, p. 1)

The focus on "reducing the psychological distance" contained in the definition of psychosocial rehabilitation is echoed in a statement by social work theorist Hans Falck.

> Membership, by definition, narrows the distance between social worker and client. The guiding concept for the social worker-client relationship is mutuality. Mutuality means that whatever is done *for* the client is done *with* the client to the greatest possible extent. (1988, p. 56)

The focus in the psychosocial rehabilitation definition on "improving ability to function in the community," "common sense," and "practical needs" lends itself to the use of classes and activity groups which promote competence in daily living skills and relationships. The use of curriculum has always been a tool in social group work. The effective use of curricula modules or any other program material necessitates that they be utilized "in the context of the professions' purposes, knowledge and skills" (Papell and Rothman, 1980, p. 20). This helps to assure that curricula is guided by member needs. With the advent of managed care and other funding agency pressures to cut costs and/or limit services, there has been a proliferation of attempts to create standardized, easily administered approaches to teaching skills that improve the ability to manage daily living tasks and relationships. It also is an understandable but simplistic response to funding authority pressures for outcome measures and deficits in staff training. In the past, good supervision was relied upon to promote learning of mutual aid practice. Today, most supervisors are not trained or skilled in the principles of mutual aid practice. Reliance on curriculum-driven practice unfortunately has become a growing trend to replace professional practice with technical application. It is fueled by the increasing availability of packaged behavioral health modules that are offered for sale under such popular descriptions as "psycho-educational" or "cognitive behavioral" materials.

Given a lack of trained social group workers in psychosocial rehabilitation agencies, there is no easy solution to this problem. It is not possible to transform paraprofessional staff into master's level social group workers. However, retraining professional staff to alter previously learned medical model approaches to share authority in their case management work with individuals has been very successful. It is also possible for social workers and other trained behavioral health professionals to learn fundamental mutual aid concepts and skills to develop a social group work mind-set to apply to their direct service and supervisory practice. Group work practice examples need to appear in the psychosocial rehabilitation literature and be utilized for training in agencies. The group work practice examples need to articulate specific psychosocial rehabilitation and mutual aid practice principles that are violated when practice is curriculum-driven.

## PRACTICE THEORY USEFUL IN MINIMIZING CURRICULUM-DRIVEN PRACTICE

Psychosocial rehabilitation agencies have historically resisted medical models of practice. The mutual aid approach of social group work offers a viable alternative. The statement in the psychosocial rehabilitation definition, "the psychosocial rehabilitation setting is purposefully informal to reduce the psychological distance between staff and members as active participants in program planning" (IAPSRS, 1985, p. 1), differentiates psychosocial rehabilitation from medical model approaches to work with groups that are based on the study-diagnose-treat model from medicine. The democratic-humanistic value base of social group work provides for an egalitarian approach that is consistent with the psychosocial rehabilitation definition. Three noted social work theories—Hans Falck's membership perspective,

William Schwartz' and Lawrence Shulman's mediating model, and Judith Lee's concept of the empowerment group—provide a framework for further discussion.

Falck describes social work practice as "rendering professional aid in the management of membership" (1988, p. 56). Falck's membership perspective theory refutes the tendency of some social work theorists who believe that there is a dichotomy between individuals and society. The membership perspective postulates a "connectedness" between all people. Falck reminds us that when working with groups, it is necessary to consider the perspectives of the many "unseen groups" that make up the membership constellation of group members. These unseen groups include family, administration, funding agencies, and the various ethnic and cultural groups people in the group belong to. Falck goes further in stating that the social worker's behavior and that of client members should be considered membership behavior, since they both operate within the overall social context. He characterizes the social worker/client membership relationship as group members "who together have the task to find solutions to problems of daily living" (p. 55). The group worker seeks to achieve this by utilizing professional skills to increase connectedness. Falck classifies qualities of membership as either: "positive," which satisfy; "negative," which alienate or "split the fact of membership from the perception of membership"; or "ambiguous," which contain both satisfying and unsatisfying elements (pp. 45-48). Falck's focus on management and improvement in the quality of membership relates well to the quality of life measures that psychosocial rehabilitation agencies profess to address as outcome measures. It is in that context that Rubin (1994) chose to incorporate a statement made by Falck describing social group work as: "a methodology of Social Work that is widely applicable for people who wish to obtain help in improving the quality of their membership with others in their various communities" (p. 284).

Judith A.B. Lee's conception of the empowerment group helps to place curriculum in social and personal perspectives by "thinking empowerment" as group workers tune in to the needs of group participants. Lee reminds us that group workers need to consciously and continually relate to issues of power and oppression when working with persons with severe mental illnesses by engaging in critical consciousness raising. This is accomplished by developing the ability to utilize "fifocal vision." Lee describes "fifocal vision" as a tool that gives the worker the "political lenses" to foster empowerment by viewing people, their behavior, and their oppressive experiences from five overlapping perspectives. The five perspectives of "fifocal vision" lenses are "historical," "ecological," "ethclass," "feminist," and "critical." Lee then promotes the utilization of the skills of "critical education" (the promotion of a critical perspective in the inquiry and learning process) and "praxis" (the process of continuous action, reflection, and then action again, rather than simple action or reflection) to engage the group in an empowerment process (1994, pp. 9, 33-36, 116-117).

Lee believes that cognitive behavioral approaches are effective in empowerment groups. This approach differs from traditional behavior modification, which has been criticized as being linear, simplistic, and mechanistic. In the empowerment group, the worker is not content with simple behavior modification or the mere achievement of empathy related to common and unique feelings and experiences. The empowerment-focused group worker seeks to maintain "critical consciousness" to help members manage feelings rather than dissipate them so that "cognitive restructuring" can occur. Cognitive restructuring consists of identifying thinking patterns, revising false beliefs, and learning more adaptive ways of dealing with realities. This approach postulates that unless a client changes the way he or she perceives and interprets experience, gains will not last. This is of prime importance in the development and utilization of structured learning materials with people who have experienced oppression. It is not enough to offer skills, facts, and knowledge to group members. Sharing of information alone does not empower people. Lee states:

> The worker's skills in guiding the process of praxis are extremely important. A worker's *feeling-oriented skills,* particularly of naming and staying with the client's feelings, are essential to this process. The ability to *promote competence and action* is also critical. Cognitive restructuring relates directly to the central skill of the empowerment approach: *consciousness raising* that postulates that oppressed people have internalized false beliefs about themselves that need to be restructured to reduce self and community blame, raise self and community esteem and take positive action. The Civil Rights Movement slogans "Power to the people," "Black is beautiful," "I'm black and I'm proud" . . . was a type of "healthier talk" that could be internalized and contribute to

basic conversation skills module, which the state-funding authority had purchased and required the agency to utilize. The agency was concerned about the effectiveness of this imposed curriculum-driven approach.

Roberta began by asking the members to help her move the tables together into a square so that people would be able to write and see each other. This took approximately five minutes. Roberta asked, "How's everyone doing?" One of the members answered, "Fine." Roberta asked the group who was missing, and two names were mentioned. There was no discussion about the missing members. Roberta asked everyone including myself to state his or her name. As I began taking notes, Mildred asked me, "Are you writing our names down?" I answered that I was writing down first names. There was no further discussion of my presence.

Roberta passed out the workbooks containing the module for the day and asked the group to tell me what the group was about. Mitch said, "Ways of communicating and getting good understanding." Roberta said, "Well put, Mitch," and did not attempt to promote discussion about what Mitch had said or elicit any additional answers. Roberta asked for volunteers to tell me about the homework assignment. Linda said, "It is to notice verbal and nonverbal communication." A second member clarified that it was to do that while observing a conversation. Roberta asked one person at a time to tell the group what they had done for the homework assignment. Mildred responded first about observing a conversation on a bus. Roberta asked if the others had any questions for Mildred. There were none. Roberta complimented Mildred on "doing very good observing" and asked the next person to report. Linda told about a conversation she had initiated. Roberta said, "You did more than observe, which was the homework assignment, you initiated a conversation. When we get to today's lesson you can share what you already did." After hearing from each member, Roberta asked whether they had become more knowledgeable about verbal and nonverbal communication from their observations. One or two members unenthusiastically said, "Yes." Roberta then said that they would go on to the lesson for the day, which was "to give examples of starting friendly conversations."

Mildred told the group about a very scary situation between a bus driver and an irate passenger that she said "scared me to death." Roberta utilized a concept from the workbook by asking Mildred if that was a "go or a no go" situation. Mildred answered, "No go." Roberta responded, "Recognizing a 'go' or 'no go' situation is a skill area in the workbook." She then instructed the group to turn to page 43 and said, "The first skill area for today is 'go or no go'." Roberta repeated that the goal for the day was "to be able to give an example of starting a friendly conversation." At that point Eva came in late from her work on the kitchen crew. Roberta welcomed her, introduced her to me, and told her where they were in the book. Roberta continued by reading from the manual that starting a friendly conversation involves learning and utilizing three skills or resources: (1) finding places where there are people to talk to; (2) identifying people who are willing to talk to you; and (3) identifying topics so you will have something to talk about. Roberta then asked individual members to read out loud from the manual. After that she asked for examples. Only Linda gave an example. Roberta accepted the answer and went on to the next section of the module. Roberta stopped after each section, asked a question, and, after receiving one answer, asked someone else to read the next section. There was no attempt to involve members in discussion with each other.

After reading the entire module, Roberta asked for comments or questions. Mildred tried to relate the three skills to a personal incident. She told about waiting in the cold for a bus with a stranger and making a joke about the weather. She said that she "felt stupid when the person didn't laugh or respond." Roberta advised, "You shouldn't feel stupid." Roberta then told them they would watch the videotape that accompanied the module and said, "Looking at this video should give you a better understanding of how to start a friendly conversation." There was a five-minute delay while Roberta and one of the members set up the tape and corrected problems with the VCR. The video repeated word for word what was written in the manual. Roberta asked questions from the manual to reinforce the three identified skills. Mildred again tried to speak authentically about her bus experience. She said, "I find it easier to talk with someone I am familiar with." Roberta acknowledged Mildred's statement but returned to the use of the video again, saying, "There is one more segment. Would someone please let me know when it is 1:25 so we don't go overtime?" The next segment of the video talked about "go" and "no go" signals. After a short video segment, Roberta pressed the pause button and asked, "If you walk into a room and there is a group in a heated discussion, is it a 'go' or a 'no go' situation?" Roberta accepted the first answer and went on to the next section of the video.

After the video, Roberta directed the group to "go to page 47" and quickly went over six guidelines for starting a conversation. When she finished she said, "Our goal for today is for everyone to be able to give an example of starting a friendly conversation. Let's go around the table." She received quick answers such as "say hi" and "talking about the weather leads to other things." After receiving the responses, Roberta asked, "Do you all feel you've reached the group goal for today?" Mildred answered, "Yes, but if someone smiles, does it give permission to start a conversation?" Roberta said, "Sometimes," and ended the group by letting the members know that they had gone five minutes overtime. I spoke with Roberta after the meeting. She said that she had been nervous being observed. She also indicated that she felt constrained by having to use the module exactly as prescribed.

## Group Workers Mistakenly Assume Responsibility for Success of the Group

In mutual aid practice, the group worker shares responsibility for leadership and authority with the group. Although the group worker does at times take on leadership functions, it is done purposefully and with care not to assume leadership functions that could be the responsibility of group members. Many common mistakes made in work with groups derive from misconceptions about the nature of leadership. One extreme is to make the mistake that leadership is the role of the worker. This results in workers assuming responsibility for the success of the group. At the other extreme is abdication of any working role with the group, which is a misinterpretation of the meaning of empowerment. This results in allowing groups to fail due to lack of social worker skill. Curriculum-driven work with a group falls into the first extreme, not sharing leadership.

Responsibility for the effectiveness of groups and meetings belongs to the group as a whole, including the group worker. Applying Falck's "membership perspective" theory, it could be argued that in the communication group that I observed, responsibility for success was assumed not just by the group worker, who utilized the prescribed curriculum, but also by several unseen groups. These unseen groups were the administration, the researchers, and the funding authorities. Lee's empowerment group work theory would explain the resistances and apathy encountered as a result of not utilizing the lenses of fifocal vision to become sensitive to authority issues and guide curriculum development. Issues related to the authority of the worker are active throughout the life of the group and need to be recognized and addressed whenever they arise.

There were numerous opportunities in this group to address the authority theme and to share responsibility with the group. One such opportunity presented itself when two names were mentioned of members who were absent. Attendance needs to be conceived of as the property of the group. Rather than the worker just reporting attendance statistics on rosters for administration or funding sources, the group could have engaged in a discussion of what to do about the two absent members. In addition to using this opportunity to reinforce the humanistic value of members being responsible for each other, it was a natural opportunity to promote sustained friendly conversation, which was the stated goal for the module for the day.

Another opportunity to deal with the authority theme was when Mildred noticed this author taking notes and asked if names were being written down. This could have led to a friendly discussion of the reason for the visit. Omission of such a discussion reinforced previous oppressive experiences common to people with severe mental illnesses whose activities and living conditions have included considerable control by institutional authorities. It would have been helpful for Roberta to recognize the anxiety behind that question and to give permission to more directly express feelings of discomfort by disclosing her own anxiety about being observed. Mildred took a great risk by initiating conversation. Her risky behavior could have been easily related to the "go or no go" concept utilized in the module. It also would have been appropriate for Roberta to seek permission about being observed in advance from the group. This would have promoted mutual aid through the recognition and sharing of feelings of being "all in the same boat." It would have helped to "reduce the psychological distance between members and staff" (IAPSRS, 1985, p. 1), and also would have been a significant opportunity to share responsibility with the group. An additional way to share responsibility for success of the group could have been to do advance planning with the group for help in setting up the room and testing the video equipment prior to the meeting. Mildred could have gained an additional

ber needs, and what the worker's role is in the group. Achievement of clarity of purpose and role are tasks for the preparation and beginning phases of work with any group. Clarification of group purpose starts with the construction of a tentative but clear statement of the agency's reason for having the group relative to what is known about the interests and developmental issues of prospective members. The work with the group involves a modification and clarification process that results in articulation of the worker role and a consensus on a statement of group purpose that is inclusive of member issues. This process is called contracting. It is a dynamic process that continues throughout the life of the group and involves continual clarification by recontracting.

Kurland and Salmon (1998, pp. 6-7) enumerate six common mistakes that group workers make in conceptualizing group purpose. Four of these common mistakes were evident in the Communications I group:

1. *Confusing group purpose with group content.* The purpose of the group was not to learn the module. Modules need to be utilized along with other resources to provide a stimulus for discussion and activity that address current group member issues.

2. *Stating group purpose too generally or too vaguely to provide direction for the group.* Both the title of the group and Mitch's statement that the group addresses "ways of communicating and getting good understanding" were examples of general descriptors often used as statements of group purpose.

3. *Viewing group purpose as static rather than dynamic.* Using a module pedagogically, as was done in this group, keeps purpose static from group to group rather than dynamic and responsive to the life experiences of group members. Group purpose needs to be accountable to the changing needs of members over the twelve weeks that each group meets. It is often necessary to recontract periodically throughout the life cycle of each group in order to make sure that the purpose remains relevant.

4. *Inadequately considering member needs.* A statement of group purpose needs to reflect the common developmental issues of people with severe mental illnesses. The statement of group purpose could vary depending on the composition of the group. For example, if the Communication I group were composed of

people living in a group home, residential relations might be the focus rather than work. For those who were experiencing difficulties with their families, the statement might include reference to communication between adults and their parents. A statement of group purpose might be: *to increase comfort and ability to participate and express ideas and feelings in (social, vocational, family and/or residential) relationships that typically cause problems for people who have experienced severe mental illnesses.*

When group purpose is established effectively, it allows psychosocial rehabilitation practitioners to justify group involvement for members by including member-specific goals rather than general goals in required member service plans.

### The Tendency for Group Workers to Do Individual Work in a Group

Shulman has identified "doing casework in a group" as a common detriment to effective practice with groups. He notes that the task of the group worker is to simultaneously pay attention to two clients, the "group as a whole," and individuals (1992, p. 401). Falck's membership perspective theory postulates that there is a "false dichotomy between individuals and society." No one can live independent of others. Falck states: "Freedom is social freedom, self-determination is social self-determination (decision making by the social self), and the social worker's role is one of holding up to clients the irreducible nature of one's sociality" (1988, p. 72). The psychosocial rehabilitation principles of fostering interdependence and relating to the larger community are consistent with Falck's statement.

The skills necessary to maintain a dual focus are complex work phase skills. An example of this problem was very evident in the Communications I group as Roberta addressed one client and one issue at a time. In curriculum-driven groups, there is often inadequate attention given to identifying common concerns, which results in doing "case work in a group." Mildred's statements and questions provided many opportunities for Roberta to depart from the module and engage the group in authentic discussions. This would have provided a more meaningful experience for the group members. Roberta needed to validate Mildred's contributions and to seek to promote/teach norms for speaking with authenticity, free-form interaction, and multi-logues. Roberta had the tendency to accept only one or two answers and move on, rather than promote discussion between members. Mutual aid evolves from such discussion.

Advice giving is another common occurrence in curriculum-driven groups. Time pressures to cover planned curricula often result in relying on module guidelines to provide an answer, which is a form of advice giving. Roberta relied on dialogues between herself and one member at a time along with what was written in the module for providing guidance to the group. This was the case when Roberta said, "You shouldn't feel embarrassed," and further advised Mildred to watch the video to get a "better idea of how to start a friendly conversation" in response to her admission of feeling embarrassed by an unsuccessful attempt to start a conversation while waiting for a bus. This would have been an excellent opportunity to support Mildred's risk in sharing her feelings by teaching and reinforcing a norm for speaking authentically. Roberta could have normalized the experience by empathizing and sharing an embarrassing attempt at conversation she had experienced. She could then have attempted to establish a pattern of free-form interaction by asking others to share similar experiences and then reflecting together on the issues involved. This would have resulted in mutual aid. It would be consistent with the psychosocial rehabilitation principles of normalizing, supporting attempts at growth, working from strengths, and fostering interdependence.

Dialogues and monologues are likely to be the pattern of communication when a group worker feels pressure to produce outcomes. If Roberta had asked the group's help in pointing out when she acts rushed and fails to promote group norms for free-form interaction, multilogue, and authenticity, she would have demonstrated the important group work values of "the worker being accountable to the group" and "individuals being responsible to one another" (Glassman and Kates, 1990, pp. 27-31, 67). It would also have helped if Roberta had asked the group to remind her to leave five or ten minutes at the end part of each meeting to accomplish evaluation and planning tasks. At that time, they could have evaluated together whether work that day was related to individual or group processes and group purpose.

## CONCLUSION

The agency in which this group occurred recognized the importance of using curriculum purposefully. After the consultation, they took steps to establish a process to more effectively address the five categories of problems identified in this chapter. Changes included:

1. Utilization of the last week of each class or activity group to do a formal evaluation of the group experience and to write a descriptive abstract to be shared during the registration for the next twelve-week session.
2. Establishment of a member/staff curriculum planning and evaluation committee that had responsibility for ongoing curriculum enhancement. This committee reviewed the evaluations of each group and the abstracts. They then determined which groups were needed for the next twelve-week session and how to enhance the curriculum. The committee did important work in trying to relate the curriculum to current membership needs. A formal evaluation process with the membership directly addresses the authority theme. It actualizes Glassman and Kates's important group work value that the worker is responsible to the group.
3. Establishment of a registration week, prior to each twelve-week session, in which case managers and members work together to choose classes and activities that best meet member interests and issues.

The author further suggests that the curriculum planning and evaluation committee include a representative from the agency research staff. This would insure that the perspectives of important unseen groups be heard and understood. Although it would not be possible to have regular participation from the funding agency that mandated the use of a prescribed curriculum, it would be a helpful strategy to invite a funding agency representative to attend one of the curriculum planning meetings. The group worker with this group could then utilize Shulman and Schwartz's mediating role to allow all perspectives to be heard and understood. This would also be consistent with Falck's membership perspective and Lee's empowerment group work practice.

The staff person who was assigned to work with the curriculum planning committee was the program director, a person with considerable authority in the agency. This was important because a major developmental issue for this planning committee was its relationship to authority. Authority can be shared more effectively when the group has access to it.

The actions initiated by this agency indicated its willingness to engage in empowerment practice. Those actions were consistent with Lee's contention that:

> Empowerment groups emerge from empowering agencies. . . . Agencies that utilize an empowerment approach to practice must be prepared to have group members react critically to the nearest environment, the agency itself. These efforts by group members signal that the process is working well and must be encouraged and welcomed. (1994, pp. 251, 258-259)

Lee's statement underscores the extent to which agencies need to be conscious of reducing psychological distance. It is consistent with the growing trend to involve recipients of service in decision-making processes at all levels of authority in the planning and delivery of psychosocial rehabilitation services.

The use of curriculum, teaching modules, and other program materials have always been an important part of group work practice. Group work is effective when mutual aid principles and skills, such as the mediating model, membership perspective, and empowerment group theory are utilized. This chapter has focused on one group example to identify common problems associated with practice that is curriculum driven. The subsequent suggestions and discussion about application of mutual aid principles and skills can be effective in promoting more purposeful practice.

## REFERENCES

Falck, H. (1988). *Social work: The membership perspective.* New York: Springer Publishing.

Glassman, U. and Kates, L. (1990). *Group work: A humanistic approach.* Newbury Park, CA: Sage Publications.

IAPSRS, (1985). *Psychosocial rehabilitation: Definition, principles and description.* Unpublished. Columbia, MD: IAPSRS.

Kurland, R. and Malekoff, A. (1998). Editorial. *Social Work with Groups 21*(1/2): 1-3.

Kurland, R. and Salmon, R. (1998). Purpose: a misunderstood and misused keystone of group work practice. *Social Work with Groups 21*(3):5-17.

Lee, J.A.B. (1994). *The empowerment approach to social work practice*. New York: Columbia University Press.

Middleman, R.R. and Goldberg-Wood, G. (1997). Constructivism, power, and social work. In Parry, J.K. (Ed.), *From prevention to wellness through group work* (pp. 1-11). Binghamton, NY: The Haworth Press, Inc.

Papell, C. and Rothman, B. (1980). Relating the mainstream model of social work with groups to group psychotherapy and the structured group approach. *Social Work with Groups 3*(2):5-23.

Rubin, M. (1994). Andrew and fellowship: Response to disaster in a psychosocial rehabilitation program: A hurricane tolerance test of structure, philosophy and methodology. In Publications Committee, IAPSRS (Ed.), *An introduction to psychiatric rehabilitation* (pp. 281-293). Columbia, MD: International Association of Psychosocial Rehabilitation Services.

Rubin, M. (2001). Knowledge and skills needed by managers and supervisors of social group work practice in agencies serving persons with severe mental illnesses. In Kelly, T., Berman-Rossi, T., and Palombo, S. (Eds.), *Strengthening resiliency through group work* (pp. 133-155). Binghamton, NY: The Haworth Press, Inc.

Schwartz, W. (1971). On the use of groups in social work practice. In Schwartz, W. and Zalba, S. (Eds.), *The practice of group work* (pp. 3-24). New York: Columbia University Press.

Shulman, L. (1992). *The skills of helping: Individuals, families and groups*. Itasca, IL: F.E. Peacock Publishers, Inc.

Steinberg, D.M. (1997). *The mutual aid approach to working with groups*. Northvale, NJ: Jason Aronson, Inc.

Toseland, R.W. and Rivas, R.F. (1995). *An introduction to group work practice*. Needham Heights, MA: Allyn & Bacon.

Treuer, E. and Rubin, M. (1993). *Direct services guide*. Miami, FL: Fellowship House.

Chapter 12

# Reflecting Extremes of Human Experience in the Group: Work with Chemically Addicted Chronic Paranoid Schizophrenic Clients

Linda Hutton

The inscription on the lintel of the Hell-Gate of Dante's Inferno reads, "Whose threshold is denied to none," and in the ninth canto the poet writes: "Through the great ward we entered unopposed/ And I being all agog to learn what state/ Of things these huge defensive works enclosed/ Gazed round, the moment I had passed the gate,/ And saw a plain, stretched spacious on both sides,/ Filled with ill woes and torments desolate" (Alighieri, 1949, p. 126). Many might describe chronic paranoid chemically addicted schizophrenic clients as having lives "filled with ill woes and torments desolate." As I crossed the agency threshold to begin my social work internship, I saw a whole range of people whose lives had been changed forever by schizophrenia, and I wondered how a neophyte social work group worker might be useful in such a setting. Using course work as a "blueprint," I found that social work with groups took on a powerful vitality and excitement. Archetypes of group dynamics unfolded, and the unique resources, powers, and initiatives of group members were discovered or rediscovered. As clients risked sharing their thoughts in the group setting, I came to see beyond the client and marveled at the psychic alchemy with which they made meaning out of chaos (Wood and Middleman, 1991).

## THE BEGINNING

I was asked to "do a group," and there was no opportunity to pre-pare or screen clients. Although some clients attended college, most were defined by the agency as "low functioning." Many suffered disabling depressions, subjective disintegration, delusions, hallucinations, frequent decompensations, and suicide attempts. All clients in the agency were required to attend groups. Usually, the leader delivered the topic in didactic fashion while group members listened passively. I began to see that these group experiences resembled closed entities; the flow of energy and information was restricted, and the group members had no interaction with their environment (Compton and Galaway, 1994). As my group work unfolded, I discovered that intense emotional reactions to discussion content caused a variety of overt behaviors. These included flights from the source of anxiety (leaving the room), or a deep, loud snoring, which was an unusual and puzzling group dynamic. Client turnover was problematic. New clients arrived, and during the year others were "graduated" to different residences. Some had doctors' appointments or came late from previously scheduled meetings. Clients typically saw the worker in other work-related situations during the week, creating the possible blurring of group boundaries and confidentiality issues. How could group work be effective in this agency setting? Where would I begin, and how could I make this experience critical, personal, integral, and responsible (Cohen, 1995)?

I was immediately influenced by the idea that groups are naturally occurring systems where the individual parts are affected by the movements of other parts (Kurland, 1978). Put another way, this "dynamic system," which contradicts the Cartesian dichotomy of mind/body philosophy, holds that the whole determines the behavior of the parts (Capra, 1982). The ability to see the group as a network of relationships was a critical component of the work. The focus was not on hierarchical relationships, which are usually imbued with power and authority, and resort to punitive measures to maintain discipline. Instead, I envisioned an open system that was self-organized, interactive with its environment, and able to create and maintain relationships and boundaries. This worldview allowed for the formation of new possibilities of self-meaning. If the group took on the risk of sharing their thoughts as the purpose for the group's existence, they would also embrace relationships, patterns, and structure as critical group elements.

## THE ENGAGEMENT

At first members were mostly silent, distant, fearful, and disinterested in any form of engagement. Some members could not whisper their own names in the group (Keefe and Harvey, 1994). It seemed to me that they felt deeply the stigma of their illness, which had been compounded by chemical addiction, homelessness, and, frequently, imprisonment. In addition, they felt convinced that their impulses and fantasies were abhorrent, a factor that seemed to further limit their interpersonal sharing (Rappoport, Reischl, and Simmerman, 1992). Many were not able to stay in the room, much less the group. Some could never sit down and were unable even to lift their eyes to look at anyone. A few left the residence and were found as far away as California. Several began to decompensate, requiring extended hospitalizations. Others relapsed, and one or two eventually gave up on the residence and returned to the streets. As I observed the apparent disintegration of the group even in its nascent stages, I questioned the likelihood of any unfolding, illumination, and transformation that is the desired expectation of the process.

Connecting related aspects of experiences, drawing upon symbolic references, trusting one's judgment, and being cognizant of the equifinality of approaches are important facets of a client-worker partnership. I looked for an appropriate and useful approach that might creatively serve as a transactional object to enhance sharing in the group. With encouragement from my supervisor, I proposed to the group that we use art as a creative medium. Because art is a symbolic form that can facilitate a different awareness of a sense of self, it can be an important nonthreatening vehicle to facilitate group interaction. Members at first declined to participate in any discussion. I continued to work toward feedback and waited patiently for "something to happen." I wanted to be flexible and to hear the clients' concerns, especially if what they wanted was not in lockstep with my own ideas. It was important also to be respectful of their defensive systems. I reminded myself that I was not there to teach or preach (Shulman, 1992).

Besides being concerned with the development of a creative approach, I paid particular attention to the structure of the group settings. Meetings were held in the same room at the same time, and we utilized the same rituals. In this setting we negotiated, renegotiated, and refined the contract often, and with all the flux and fluidity of an ocean's tide (Wood and Middleman, 1991). For example, instead of requiring clients to remain in the room, I decided to utilize the Milan Associates paradoxical approach. I invited those who found the group experience difficult to freely leave the room (Nichols and Schwartz, 1998). Only rarely did clients leave. When they did, they told the group what was going on that made it necessary for them to take a break. Often, they would simply and powerfully say, "I have to collect myself." This was different from their other group experiences where members risked punishment if they violated the mandate to stay in the room.

Another important feature in the beginning process was the identification of emerging content themes and process themes. Teasing out these themes brought coherence to the process and indicated to the group that I paid close attention to what was going on (Phillips and Markowitz, 1989). I found that when I linked the work of previous meetings with the present one, members were pleased that their words had been taken seriously; the process was responsive, and a deeper sense of involvement began to occur.

Techniques such as tuning in, empathetic responses, observation of body language, and persistent encouragement were helpful in coaxing members to participate in the group. Gradually, the room became a safer place, and members started to speak. We stayed with the issue of art for several sessions. Eventually, very strong opinions concerning the group's use of art, which they angrily described as childish, emerged. As an alternative, and using solutions from Mazza and Price (1985), I suggested working with poetry, myth, or storytelling, all of which appealed to group members. We agreed that the group's designated purpose would be to become more comfortable in sharing our thoughts and feelings in the group setting.

## THE GROUP PROCESS

The selection of poems or myths became both a collaborative and directed process. Sometimes members made special requests, such as poetry by African-American poets. Often we chose selected short myths or chapters from a particular book. Members used these readings in different ways. I noticed that the meaningful use of language and the experience of being read to had important soothing and relaxing effects for group members. These were significant benefits since most clients came to the group in a state of high anxiety and stress from excessive external stimuli. At approximately the twelfth group meeting, some members asked me to read from *The Adventures of Tom Sawyer.* After such a reading, the first group sharing of personal experiences occurred.

RICH*: I just keep waiting for the adventure to begin.

JESSE: Yes. It's interesting that the adventure hasn't started yet.

RICH: I guess it's like life. When I was growing up I couldn't wait to be all grown up. Then when I was grown up I couldn't believe how hard it is to be grown up.

LOIS: That's exactly right. It's easy when everything is done for you when you are young.

JESSE: Rich is exactly right. We keep waiting for the adventure to begin. I think we have to slow down a bit.

DORA: We are just finding out what kind of a person Tom is. I think he is naughty. I kinda like him! He does mean things, and sometimes he gets into trouble, but I like him!

LOIS: I think the same thing. He gets in trouble, but it's sort of exciting.

TERRY: I guess that's right. I lived like that with substance abuse an' all. Now it's different. But I still think of the excitement I felt then. Now I am learning to live without the excitement and the adventure.

JESSE: It's hard work, but you get to know yourself better.

For most group members, secrecy was an especially important and isolating factor in their lives. Their illness was a cause for extreme embarrassment; their drug addiction was a cause for deep shame and guilt. As they became able to and comfortable with expressing their similarity to others, they began to understand their shared histories. An increased cohesiveness and an *esprit de corps* slowly emerged in

---

*All client names in this chapter have been changed.

the group. It was an unfolding and transforming process both for the clients and for myself. I had initially felt their isolation as rejection, their unresponsiveness as anger, and their fearfulness as a reflection of my inexperience and clumsiness. As Kurland and Salmon state eloquently, "Group work is a method of working with people that is affirming of their strengths and of their ability to contribute to others" (1992, p. 12).

## MUTUAL AID

Gradually, I became better able to facilitate feedback within the group, and we moved further into the process. We relied more on our relationships with one another in the here and now, and we built on the mutual aid concept "we are all in this together" (Germain and Gitterman, 1996, p. 242). As a result, I saw meaningful self-disclosures grow from abstract theoretical concepts into oscillating, living archetypes of group dynamics. I noticed that when members risked sharing their thoughts, their sense of isolation decreased. This was a very potent and observable outcome of the work. Another outcome was that communication skills improved and members began to help each other in noncritical, nonjudgmental ways. For example, Dora always directed her questions to me and looked to me for the answers to her problems. I was drawn very strongly to focus attention on her and grant her wish for individual attention. On one occasion, she turned to me and explained that her mother didn't want her to go home for Christmas. Dora was very upset, and I looked for ways to involve the group in the process.

DORA: I'd like to go. I don't know what's wrong with my mother. Maybe she hates me.

WORKER: Have you asked her what's going on?

DORA: No, I haven't. I just know she hates me.

WORKER: Sometimes it is very hard for families to understand schizophrenia. I wonder if she is afraid of the mental illness. What does the group think?

JESSE: Yeah. People think we do crazy stuff all the time. People have to be educated.

DORA: How would I educate her?

NICK: Holidays are bad times for me too. Everyone drinks at Christmas time. It scares me. I think we should talk about this.

WORKER: Well, let's do that and see if we can form some plan of action that helps everyone.

DORA: Could we do that?

JESSE: Yeah, we could get information about schizophrenia and show it to her.

The whole group became involved in the process through the use of techniques such as scanning, directing members' transactions toward one another, and inviting members to build on one another's contributions (Germain and Gitterman, 1996). This *in vivo* discussion promoted a more open attitude about mental illness, substance abuse, families, and vacation times. Empowering families of the mentally ill became the theme of the discussion. The idea that some families blame themselves for such illnesses evoked very touching disclosures from several members (Lee, 1994). While writing my process notes, I thought that Dora might have also been talking about me, the mother figure in the group. This raised the important issue of appropriately identifying latent and manifest material in the group context. Transference does occur in groups, and either ignoring it or confusing it can mislead the group (Yalom, 1995).

Members became personally interested in the work and gradually started to organize how they wanted the group to be. We had a specific ritual for the beginning and ending of each session. We lit a candle to signal the beginning and followed with a short meditation and a few moments of silence. We always wound the meeting down by reviewing the prevailing themes of the session. The level of trust and safety that the members embraced in order to sit in silence in a semi-darkened room was an exceptional effort. Within the framework of these group sessions, members started to be more revealing in their personal disclosures. Following another reading from *Tom Sawyer* in which Tom, Joe, and Huck steal food and run away to the island, the following dialogue took place:

JESSE: I feel embarrassed. This makes me feel bad.

NICK: Why is that?

JESSE: Well, you know I did a lot of stuff like that, stealing and stuff, and I am not proud of it. In fact, the story makes me remember a lot of embarrassing stuff I did when I was younger.

WALT: We all did stuff like that, man. That's what kids do. It's kinda embarrassing, but it's what kids do.

RICH: Yeah, we all done that stuff. The running away bit is like what I do all the time, you know. I still run away from myself just hoping that I can leave my problems behind. But it don't happen like that.

WORKER: This is powerful stuff for the group. There are a lot of strong reactions here. How did you react, Lois? You seem a bit quiet today.

LOIS: I was thinking that my little two year old tells me he will run away if he don't get what he wants. (Laughs.) I ran away. I think I sometimes run away now. But I am back on the right track now, and it feels real good.

## *BEHAVIOR IN THE GROUP*

During all agency group meetings, a puzzling snoring phenomenon took place. Serena made a "snoring" noise so loudly that group members could not hear themselves. She feigned sleep but was seldom truly asleep. The pattern of behavior was predictable. Five minutes into the group's work, Serena began to snore. The *mise en scene* between the worker and the client was also clear and predictable. The group leader usually expressed frustration, resentment, and anger by staring at Serena, raising her eyebrows, physically shaking Serena, and shouting at her to "wake up." On several occasions, the leader expelled her from the group, an indication perhaps of empathic failure. I thought that this Pyrrhic victory deprived the group of basic cohesiveness. Expelling her may also have affirmed for Serena that no one understood her. Other members appeared "glazed over" or "zoned out." They appeared externally calm, manifesting, I thought, a strong self-protective action that surely belied internal discomfort. Members probably experienced an increased sense of impotence and despair. It also appeared that trust and faith in the group process may have suffered when repetitive, predictable Band-Aid solutions to the problem were enforced.

I wondered how I should interpret and manage this signal to advance the work of the group. I hypothesized that it was a group issue, and not an individual one, that begged for group exploration. It was possible that the group had scapegoated Serena and permitted her "monopolize" the group because it served a prevailing group solution. The second important factor was that this was a group crisis, an impasse that obstructed further advancement.

During this crisis time, I became aware that I was waking myself up in the middle of the night by my own snoring. I am not usually a snorer and was perplexed by this new behavior. I wondered if I were developing some kind of apnea, since I seemed to gasp for air when I awoke. In the course of writing in my journal, I linked my own bizarre episodic "snoring" to what was happening in the group. Was there something important that I was actively avoiding? What was it that I must "wake up to"? Was I afraid I might awake to find myself in "a dark wood,/ Where the right road was wholly lost and gone" (Alighieri, p. 71)? How was I participating in the group snoring choreography? I felt at the outset that I was in the midst of an experience that had a very strong affective component with important significance for the whole group. These were profound countertransferential experiences.

As the snoring client continued her loud signals in our group, I felt more and more defensive. I ignored the snoring noise. Because I took no action (a deprature from my usual strategy in other groups I led), I began to experience a higher degree of tension in the group. As Shulman says, "When the group is operating, one can see group members translating their thoughts and feelings into actions that adapt to reality" (1992, p. 505). Members became more silent and passive. Some left the room declaring they "needed to collect" themselves. I continued to affirm, reframe, and go beyond the behavior, and as we discussed a myth that had been particularly engaging for everyone, the anamorphosis or trajectory toward a different level of functioning occurred.

NICK: A lot of myths have this central theme of an inner journey.

WORKER: How does the group feel about this idea of being on a journey?

WALT: Well, we are trying to get it together so we can get our own places. That's the goal, the journey. Can you tell Serena to stop snoring? It's very irritating and disruptive.

WORKER: What would happen if you told her, Walt?

WALT: Oh no, I can't do that.

WORKER: Well, what do you think might happen if you did?

WALT: We're not supposed to. She would fight and be mad. But you have to. You're the leader. You have to tell her. It's disruptive, isn't it? Don't you think it is irritating?

WORKER: Yes, I think it is disruptive. What does the group think?

NICK: Well, everyone tells her to stop, but she does it all the time.

WALT: You have to go and tell the director. She knows what to do. It's disrespectful, isn't it?

NICK: The same thing happens over and over again.

JESSE: You have to do something.

WORKER: Let me see if I understand this. The group does not like Serena snoring. You have strong feelings about it. The solutions that have been used so far all produce the same result, which seems to be no change. You say you can actually predict what will happen every time. Someone will wake Serena up and tell her not to snore, and she will fall back and snore again. Is that right?

NICK: Yes. It's a predictable pattern. The solution we have doesn't work.

WORKER: Well, does the group have some ideas of how we can solve the problem?

WALT: It's not up to us, Linda! It's up to you! You are the leader. It is your group. You have to tell her.

WORKER: Well, Walt, I have a problem with that idea. I feel that the group belongs to the group. The solution everyone has tried before is not working. Is it possible for us to think about different ways to solve the problem?

WALT: You are too soft, Linda!

WORKER: I hear you. You think I should stop the snoring. It seems that this is a very important and difficult issue for the group. I don't have any answers for this problem. What can we do about it together?

JESSE: I think we have to just go on with the story. Ignore her.

Although I recognized the group's dependency as a form of avoiding the real work, I could not avoid my own feelings of inadequacy. I was affected by the strength of anxiety in the group and wondered if I could stay with the emotion. This type of collaboration was a new experience for the group, and for me too. The prevailing question was whether my demand for work was realistic. I felt it was important that I avoid any restrictive solutions that might make me feel better but would cause the group to revert to previous maladaptive behavior. During subsequent group meetings, I continued to mirror the group's behavior: I ignored the snoring. However, as I read poetry or myths, I provocatively lowered my voice. The louder the snoring noise became, the softer my voice became. Finally, a client spoke out, saying to me, "Linda, you have to do something about the disruptive noise." I turned it back to the group, and for the first time we began a serious group discussion about the snoring problem.

Some group members suggested that we send Serena out of the room. It was a proposal that sparked a lively debate regarding the concept of mutual aid. In the end, the group reasoned that we should all try to help Serena stay in the group. However, no one had any thoughts on how we might accomplish this. Serena, who always came to group meetings, sat with her eyes closed but made no loud snoring noises while discussions of the problem occurred. The difference now was that the snoring was no longer painfully ignored or tolerated by the group. I could see that all the members had become engaged in a "struggle between the group's primitive instincts to avoid the pain of growth and its need to become more sophisticated and deal with feelings" (Shulman, 1992, p. 505).

At the next meeting, Terry spoke directly to Serena. "Serena," he said, "you have to stop this loud noise because we can't have our group." Other group members looked with mixed, apprehensive glances at Terry, who continued to exhort Serena to "come into the group." Soon other group members joined him and encouraged Serena to make a commitment to the group. This time, Serena responded positively. She began to participate in group discussions. She did not snore during meetings again. Unfortunately, the snoring conundrum remained unsolved, since another client invariably assumed that duty. However, the group had taken a giant risk and dealt with their feelings openly. They confronted a very difficult group issue in a way that had not been experienced previously. In the process, they depended less on authority (the worker) for solutions to problems.

## THE ENDING

In the final weeks, the group took on the issue of schizophrenia when Jesse said, "We have no trouble coming up with negative stuff about this illness. I'd like for us to think of something positive about schizophrenia." They cautiously identified their strengths, such as optimism and resiliency. They spoke of their hopes for the future and their dogged determination to take on their difficulties one day at a time. To illustrate their feelings about their illness, they decided to write a group poem, which would be our parting gift to each other. During the last six meetings I collected words and ideas from each person in the group. Some had wanted to write their own poems, but in another important disclosure, Jesse told the group he did not know how to read or write and could we find another way for him to partici- pate. Terry, encouraged by the shared admission, revealed his own embarrassment concerning his illiteracy and asked if I would write for the group. I found large white sheets of paper and fastened them to the walls of the room. There, as we hashed out themes, ideas, and words, I wrote them on the wall hangings, often misspelling words and asking for help from the group. It became a vital, enthusiastic collaborative effort.

I began the ending process six sessions prior to leaving by simply informing the group that we had six more sessions left. The group re- acted with a brief silence before shifting to another topic. However, the reaction during the following session was more dramatic. They fell silent. I noticed that everyone had their eyes closed. I waited, and after approximately two or three minutes, the following interaction took place:

JESSE: We are not angry at you, Linda. We are not sleeping. We have other things on our minds today. We got no money yet. It's late to- day, and it makes me feel kinda bad.

WORKER: Is that what's happening here?

RICH: Yeah, I feel gloomy.

WORKER: What other feelings are there here?

NICK: Oh, a lot, but having no money is the worst feeling. Like I have no power. But I remember when I had a lot of money. It is funny, I was very unhappy then too, but that may have been because of my illness.

TOM (new client): I have anxiety when I have no money.

JESSE: I feel very depressed and helpless.

NICK: I was thinking just now about feeling bad about the years I was ill. It was such a waste. It was a loss for me. A big loss in my life. I am doing much better now, but I feel angry about that. Schizophrenia, you know, it takes away so much.

JESSE: I was thinking about the time I worked in construction. I hope I can go back to work someday. (Pause.) I was thinking about the poem and the things you read. I didn't understand a lot of it, but it sort of made sense to me. (Pause.) We will miss this group. It's different and kinda sets us up to handle the other groups. The meditation is good too. We work with problems different here. But we have had interns here before, and they move on, and we can relax in the summer and go outside more and have more fun. Change isn't so bad.

During these last several sessions, we spoke about the natural cycle of bereavement and the many ways we navigate ourselves through personal losses. Together we designed a series of ritualistic endings that the group decided were meaningful. One of my last journal entries read:

> One farewell celebration that the group wanted to organize was a picnic in Central Park. I had concerns about this. I had never taken the group outside the confines of the meeting room, how would I manage such a trip? However, encouraged by the group's optimism I began to organize the trip. It was a beautiful day in May when we set out on our way to John Lennon's Strawberry Fields sanctuary in Central Park. Along the way some group members told stories about how they played there as children; some had spent their lives near Central Park and some had lived as homeless people there. I remembered my initial reactions, nine months ago, when I first met these clients. I had been variously repulsed, fearful or overwhelmed. Now as we shared a picnic on the fresh green grass under a clear blue sky, I was overcome with emotion. Most of all, I could scarcely believe how harshly I had once judged these brave people. Imagine.

We also scheduled a closing "fire ceremony," during which we would burn the one thing we most desired to be rid of. Some members said they would burn their anxiety or their anger or their harsh judging selves or schizophrenia itself. We also wanted to memorialize something of value that we had learned from the group. Some spoke of the peace they experienced or the ability to relax or the ability to solve problems or relate to others in a different way. However, the rain came in relentless torrents, and the fire ceremony was cancelled. Instead, Dora prepared an impromptu skit in which she sashayed into the room and imitated me lighting a candle and reading a poem. At the very end, we read the poem the group had written on schizophrenia.

> Lonely Seagull
> Be still lonely bird
> Break the chains and socialize
> Soothing ambition is not far away
> Thank God I am here to day.
> War and death are only confusion
> We love you, lonely seagull.
>
> Sweet serenity will medicate your misfortune
> As you soar beyond the bridge
> Towards enlightenment from mystification.
> Rehabilitation will guide you to happiness.
> War and death are only confusion
> We love you lonely seagull.

The vast plain that had stretched so ominously before me when I entered the gate to begin the internship was still full of woes and torments. At the end, however, despite "huge defensive works," the group members had come to creatively express themselves, sharing their thoughts and hopes and relying on each other for support. In the process we came to understand our strengths, our hopes, and our interdependence, notions that transcend all populations.

## REFERENCES

Alighieri, D. (1949). *The Divine Comedy. Cantica 1: Hell* (Trans. D. Sayers). New York: Penguin Books.
Capra, F. (1982). *The Web of Life*. New York: Anchor Books Doubleday.
Cohen, C. (1995). Making it Happen: From Great Ideal to Successful Support Program. *Social Work with Groups* 18(1):67-80

Compton, B.R. and Galaway, B. (1994). *Social Work Processes.* Pacific Grove, CA: Brooks/Cole.

Germain, C.B. and Gitterman, A. (1996). *The Life Model of Social Work Practice.* New York: Columbia University Press.

Keefe, R.S. and Harvey, P.D. (1994). *Understanding Schizophrenia.* New York: The Free Press.

Kurland, R. (1978). Planning: The Neglected Component of Group Development. *Social Work with Groups* 1(2):173-178.

Kurland, R. and Salmon, R. (1992). Group Work versus Casework in a Group: Principles and Implications for Teaching and Practice. *Social Work with Groups* 15(4):3-14.

Lee, J. (1994). *The Empowerment Approach to Social Work Practice.* New York: Columbia University Press.

Mazza, N. and Price, B. (1985). When Time Counts: Poetry and Music in Short-Term Group Treatment. *Social Work with Groups* 8(2):53-66.

Nichols, M.P. and Schwartz, R.C. (1998). *Family Therapy, Concepts and Methods.* Boston: Allyn & Bacon.

Phillips, M.H. and Markowitz, M.A. (1989). The Mutual Aid Model of Group Services. *Experiences of New York Archdioceses Drug Abuse Prevention Program.* Fordham University Graduate School of Social Services. Unpublished report.

Rappoport, J., Reischl, M., and Zimmerman, M. (1992). Mutual Help Mechanisms in Empowerment of Former Health Patients. In Saleeby, D. (Ed.), *The Strengths Perspectives in Social Work Practice* (pp. 84-97). New York: Longman.

Shulman, L. (1992). *The Skills of Helping: Individuals, Families and Groups.* Itasca, IL: F.E. Peacock.

Wood, G.G. and Middleman, R.R. (1991). Advocacy and Social Action: Key Elements in the Structural Approach to Direct Practice in Social Work. *Social Work with Groups* 14(3/4):53-63.

Yalom, I.D. (1995). *The Theory and Practice of Group Psychotherapy.* New York: Basic Books.

# Index